The Complete FSOT Study Guide

FSOT PRACTICE TESTS AND PREPARATION GUIDE
FOR THE WRITTEN EXAM AND ORAL ASSESSMENT

Robert Clark

Aegis Group LLC

The Complete FSOT Study Guide
Copyright © 2016 by Aegis Group LLC

Disclaimer

Every effort has been made to ensure that the content provided on this book is accurate and helpful for our readers at the time of publishing. However, this is not an exhaustive treatment of the subjects and as you probably know, the Department of State could change their testing practice or layout to the FSO selection process at any moment. No liability is assumed for losses or damages due to the information provided. You are responsible for your own choices, actions, and results.

To those out in the field and foreign deployed, I salute you for your continued vigilance, dedication, and most importantly, your service.

Contents

INTRODUCTION

In more than a decade of service, I have seen many Foreign Service Officers (FSOs) with different backgrounds ranging from teachers, students, firefighters, and plumbers to even video store clerks. It's actually quite hard to label who is destined to succeed as a Diplomat and who isn't based on their background. One of the greatest diplomats I've ever worked with was a Barnes and Noble clerk who played Dungeons and Dragons before he decided to become an FSO.

This isn't to say D&D players make the best diplomats, but there's no such thing as a prototypical FSO. Just because you already have your Master's Degree in International Relations or only just finished college with a degree in something unrelated like physics—which is where I was when I began—being selected to become a Foreign Service Officer is a challenge and requires the utmost in preparation.

A Diplomat has to have a vast wealth of knowledge on a multitude of different subjects such as math, social science, international relations, history, etc. However, they must also possess incredible communication skills, negotiations capability, and carry themselves in a manner most fitting for the title of "Diplomat." In order to find the right person with all of these qualities and capabilities, the State Department designed the Foreign Service Officer selection process to discover exactly that.

As you can imagine, finding people who exude the above qualifications, capabilities, and knowledge is extremely hard. Over the years, it's been averaged that twenty to forty percent pass the Foreign Service Officer Test, the first stage of the selection process, and out of that, only twenty to thirty percent pass the Oral Examination, the final stage. As a result, that brings us to a staggeringly low number of only around ten percent who actually become Foreign Service Officers.

From experience, I will tell you that this number shouldn't intimidate you. A majority of the people in those statistics fail because they never go all the way through with it, or they quit midway. While preparing for the process or waiting for the results, people's lives and situations change. That could include marriage, having children, a promotion at a new job, or just a change in direction. Either way, many people who start the process never see it all the way through.

Another large portion of the failures come from those who believe they don't need to prepare. I have met many potential hopefuls who told me they should be absolutely fine because they studied politics in school, and "do great in jeopardy." Don't believe me? I really have heard that in a couple of situations. These people believe they have what it takes from the get-go and will be fine. However, they learn later that they don't.

Then, there are those who take this very seriously and understand that even though they may have a strong background, to become a great FSO, they will always need to study, prepare, and grow. It's ingrained in their lifestyle and is usually the unifying factor between all who pass and go on to lead successful careers in the Foreign Service.

To tell you the truth, ever since I started the process years ago, I haven't stopped studying or developing even after becoming a Diplomat. As a part of my normal routine and on my way to the embassy, I usually have two local newspapers tucked under my arms and my Kindle stocked with downloads of the latest academic journal and non-fiction books stuffed in a pocket.

My point is, to truly become an effective Diplomat in the service of the United States, you need to constantly prepare and grow. Your knowledge on the new Chinese economic policy may be of use, even if you are stationed in Botswana. This sort of mentality needs to be cultivated from the beginning.

Considering that you are currently holding this book in your hands, I think it's fair to say you belong to the right group, and I truly commend you for that. It's important that you understand that the best FSOs I've ever worked with are the ones who are always on a search for knowledge and ready for whatever challenge the job may present no matter how busy their lives seem to get.

But how does one prepare for such a task? How does someone exude the right criteria and beat the odds?

Well, that's the point of this book …

STRUCTURE OF THIS GUIDE

My ultimate objective is to not waste your time, but instead make you more effective and efficient in your FSOT preparations, while also sharing with you things that may have a direct effect on your success in the FSO selection process.

To do this, I'll first give you a brief overview of the selection process as a whole. I'll give you practical tips for the different steps you'll have to take and information you won't find anywhere else. Having been a Diplomat and served with FSOs of all generations, I have been privy to the changes of the selection process as well as those who have administered it. This means I'm in the perfect position to help you prepare for each step in the selection process and will show you things you probably didn't know that graders do or look at in the FSO selection process.

On top of that, I will give you some inside information on a topic many sites and study guides fail to cover: the Security and Medical Clearance checks. Although they are the last step in the process, they are extremely important. More people than you think fail these and could have known they would fail them if someone had just told them a little bit more before they started the application process. I'll not only cover those areas in depth but will also give you some guidance on how to pass, as well as quicken the process. Furthermore, I'll discuss one thing that is absolutely killing current, young applicants without them realizing it.

Next, we'll move onto preparing for the FSOT by discovering where you stand. As the FSOT consists of multiple subjects that range from economics to current events, it's important to know in which areas your weaknesses lie. I've designed this pretest in such a way that once you are finished and you tally your scores, you will have an indication of exactly what subjects you need to focus on the most. This should help you put together a study plan and assist you in improving upon your weaknesses.

Upon completion of your pretest, I'll give you a list of recommended reading and discuss what you can gloss over and where you can cut corners. I'll also hand you some other methods to efficiently work through the study material. If you were to take the recommendations of the State Department's website, you would need to read more than 46,000 pages. I'll show you how to acquire the knowledge you need in far less and how to digest this information while not adding to your already busy lives.

However, this isn't just about passing the FSOT. Like I mentioned before, in order to become a great FSO, you'll need to cultivate a study plan and approach that you'll carry with you as you progress through the ranks in the FSO community. That's why I'll show you my routine and what worked for me so you can understand what you'll need to setup in order to pass and be successful in your new profession.

To further help you with that, I'll discuss all sections of the FSOT in detail. I'll explain their formats, give you tips on how best to prepare for each section, and share practical information on taking the exam that only someone who has taken it himself can share.

To cap off your FSOT preparation, I'll give you a complete practice test. This test should be used as a gauge of your current level and another means to decide which areas you still need to focus on more. My hope is that if you felt confident with the practice test, you'll be ready for the official test. However, understand that passing the practice test does not guarantee you'll pass the official test. It only serves as an indication.

Lastly, I put together a complete list of resources for you that you should take advantage of for your test *and* for your future progression as an FSO. Your education and preparation does not stop when you're hired, but it will be something you'll need to continue as you move forward.

After years of helping other potential FSOs, the above information should suffice to dramatically help your chances to succeed. Again, these are things I wish someone had told me before I began my journey as a Diplomat, and I have been told by those I helped that the information was invaluable.

SETTING THE RIGHT EXPECTATIONS

Now, by no means do I want you to think that this is the only study material you'll need or that just by reading this one book, you will be able to march right into the test room and become the next great Diplomat of our time. But like any good study guide, I'm here to tell you where you can cut corners, save time, and understand things that no state government website will tell you.

The problem with most materials that exist on this subject is that they are written in a formulaic manner and in most cases repeat things that you can find on the official State website. The truth is, neither the State website nor renditions of it will help you become more competitive. It's important to know the facts about the test. However, after having read it once, reading it again will cost you valuable time, and in most cases, this gives you no sustenance in which to improve upon.

Starting to see why most fail?

To help streamline this process, I will only restate facts when I believe there is a reason to. If I go into details on something you could find online, understand that it is of grave importance, or I will extend upon this so as to show you something you haven't seen, to include examples, different views, and experience on the subject.

It is my expectation that the reader of this guide has explored the State's official FSOT website because I do not intend to waste your time.

My hope is that upon finishing this study guide, you will have an in-depth knowledge beyond what you can find elsewhere and will be better prepared than your peers so that you will be a part of that ten percent that will join me in the international political arena.

So, with that, let's begin.

THE FOREIGN SERVICE OFFICER SELECTION PROCESS

The Foreign Service Officer (FSO) selection process consists of several steps, of which the FSOT is only one small part. That's important to realize before you get started, because once you start the FSO selection process, you must pass all steps before you can become an FSO. If you don't, you have to wait twelve months and start the process all over again-including anything you already passed.

In this first chapter, I'll discuss the different steps of the FSO application process which include:

- Medical and Security Clearance: what you need to know even before registering
- Passing the Security Clearance
- Choosing a career track
- How to register for the Foreign Service Officer Test (FSOT)
- Practical considerations when taking the FSOT
- Taking the Qualifications Evaluation Panel (QEP)
- Taking the Oral Assessment (FSOA)
- Passing the Suitability Review Panel
- How to acquire bonus points
- The Immediate Conditional Offer
- The Register

If you are already familiar with these or are in a hurry and just want to study for the FSOT, feel free to skip to the next chapter. **However**, like I said in the introduction, my goal is not to rehash previous information and thus waste your time. Instead, each point above has necessary factual information and includes analysis and findings based on experience on both sides of the process: being an FSO potential and FSO tester.

You'll notice that I am starting out of order on this. There is an important reason why.

FSOT TEST REQUIREMENTS

As you're reading this book in preparation for the FSOT, you've probably already verified you meet the requirements listed on the U.S. State Department's website.

However, those are not all the requirements that have to be met if you want to become a Foreign Service Officer. After having passed the different tests of the application process (including the FSOT), applicants must go through a medical and security clearance. This is mentioned in the eligibility requirements for the FSOT, but without any further explanation, and in many cases, these can be clear career killers.

As someone who passed both clearances, I think it's crucial that you know what they consist of even before you register and start preparing for the FSOT. Too many candidates see the Security and Medical Clearance as something they don't need to worry about until after they've successfully taken the other steps to become an FSO.

They're mistaken. If you are not one hundred percent sure that you have what it takes to pass these two clearances, chances are you'll fail them and all your work will have been for nothing. You can fail the FSOT and take it again a year later, but if you're not physically qualified to become an FSO, or if you're seen as a security threat, there's no second chance ... and believe me, these two are very strict.

It amazes me how many people begin the FSO selection process but fail to look at the big picture—becoming a diplomat. Before the U.S. government will send you across the world to represent the United States in high-level negotiations and discussions, they will need to ensure you are capable of handling such rigorous tasking and will maintain a level of integrity at all times. It will be a complete waste of money and time if they select you and find out later that you are incapable of handling secret material or living in a place like Sierra Leone due to some dependency on medical assistance or drugs—even common ones. For you to join the ranks, the government needs to know they can send you to the farthest reaches of the planet and you can be trusted.

So, let's look into these two critical steps before moving on. Do not overlook them like many have in the past.

The Security Clearance

The security check was created to ensure that you don't have anything in your past that would cause the U.S. government not to trust you. Upon getting to this step, they will hire a private investigator (through a contracted company) to access your records and learn as much about you as possible. You'll be required to fill out an incredible amount of information, and the investigator will hold you to it.

A friend of mine had the distinct non-pleasure of learning about the government's background check. In his case, his father was a missionary, and when he was little, he and his parents moved to Colombia. While there, his little brother was born, and he went on to have an incredible experience moving from country to country. He was fluent in more than seven different languages and had a sense of culture that was unparalleled to anyone else's.

However, upon entering his security check for the FSO process, he was stopped. When looking at his records, they found that his brother, who was nine at the time, was Colombian. This sparked a whole new investigation causing him and his family a major headache. My friend finally did pass, but it cost him an extra six months. That headache could have been prevented, if only he had become sensitive to the needs of the investigator during his security check.

Although it may sound ridiculous having your nine-year-old little brother stop your accession into the diplomatic world because he is "Colombian," understand that this could have been mitigated or made easier if my friend had understood this concept and informed the investigator from the beginning.

But who would have thought to point that out? Hopefully you will after finishing this.

Conditions to think about

Let me begin this section by pointing out that this is not meant to be seen as racist, ethnocentric, or even condescending toward other cultures. But please bear in mind that many countries hold a higher risk for security and will cause issues along the way.

Therefore, before you get to the security clearance check, here are some things you should think about.

a. Are you married or related to a foreign national?
b. Is that foreign national someone from a high-risk country like China, Russia, etc.?
c. Do you know every location that you have lived in over the past ten years (e.g., full addresses)?
d. Do you have proof of this?
e. Is there a person or contact for each place who will vouch for you living there that isn't a relative?

    f.   Have you ever had any altercations with the law?

    g.   Any criminal records?

    h.   How much debt do you have?

    i.   Have you ever foreclosed on a house?

    j.   How is your social media footprint? (We'll discuss this later in the chapter.)

    k.   Do you have any history of being a part of divisive groups (including violent protests, rallies, or anything else that would or could be construed as divisive in nature)?

Just because you may display some of the above criteria, it doesn't mean you will not pass the security check. However, it does mean that you should be sensitive to this and be as upfront about it as possible. Also, in some cases, you can start to prepare paperwork and proof in anticipation for your security check interview, if you make it to that step in the FSO selection process.

Ways to improve the process

Although I can't help you lie or change your records, I will say there are key things you can do that will make your investigation go more smoothly and prevent you from that same situation as my friend had … even if your little brother is Colombian.

1.   Immediately start collecting data on your previous homes and locations. Ensure that you have no gaps and that you have the full version of all of your addresses.

2.   Ensure you have two personnel that are not family members who can vouch that you lived in each place. You'll need different people for each location.

3.   When having someone vouch for your location, ensure they understand an investigator will be contacting them—and they really will. Also ensure they are prepared for the conversation. The investigator will ask questions like "Is the person trustworthy?" or "Have you ever seen the person do something that was questionable?" Personally, I had someone from my college years tell me they were going to put me down for that time period. I recommended they not put me down because I knew that if they asked about a drinking problem, I would have to answer honestly. Ensure they understand this because one wrong person can add extra months to your investigation.

4.   We'll go into social media later, but suffice it to say that your Facebook profile and other social media areas should be cleaned up.

5.   Get a credit report and check to verify you don't have any major marks. If you do, fix them. It's okay to have loans, but ensure that your loan-to-income ratio is somewhat low. You don't want to be seen as a financial risk.

6. Do a Google search for your name, and check to see what comes up. Was there a news article about you in college or pictures of you doing something you wouldn't want an investigator to see? If so, then a potential fix is to send a DCMA takedown notice to that website's server and force the material to no longer show. To learn how to do this, go here: https://nppa.org/page/5617

7. Identify any potential problems from the beginning, and ensure that it is annotated in your form. Be upfront about it. If the investigator finds out on with you telling them, they will be even more cautious about your information and perform even more in-depth searches into basic knowledge.

Social Media and Online Footprints

Prior to 2003, social media was almost nonexistent. There was no such thing as Facebook status updates, tweets, social bookmarking, etc. However, over the course of a couple of years, people have started creating what is called an "online footprint." With the invention of Facebook and Twitter, people started publishing embarrassing pictures, political views, and their personal data. By doing this, they create a clear window for potential employers and strangers to look into and pass judgment.

Everyone's social footprint is different. Some of you might be new to the game of social media and therefore lack an online presence, while others might have been a part of social media since its inception and have years of data about themselves floating around in Internet space.

Regardless of the extent of your social footprint, it is absolutely necessary that you conduct a scrub of your online presence and ensure the existing data online is the type of information you would want to be seen by potential employers or—in this case—the Foreign Service Officers or the investigator. Your online footprint and what it says about you is becoming more important every year and is playing a major factor in the selection process.

For the investigator doing your security clearance check, your social media profile can give them some valuable information. Depending on your privacy settings, people can look at your profile and can see what you like, what you do on the weekends, where you go, etc. They can access past pictures and see if you are doing things that would compromise your integrity.

For the State Department, your online footprint is extremely important because it helps them to see who you really are, not just who you are in an interview. It gives them an ability to ensure you don't have a drinking problem, aren't overbearing in political views, or have anything that would call your character into question. Remember that if you are selected as an FSO, you will always be a direct representative of the U.S. Government. This representation includes your home life and your social life. If you are implicated for some sort of issue, the news won't report it as "Mr. or Mrs. So-And-So conducted a specific action," but instead it will be reported as "An official of the U.S. State Department did the following." This can have regional and international effects that can be detrimental to the overall goal of the U.S. Government.

Furthermore, social media has become an increasingly useful tool for foreign governments to use as a means in which to develop coercive measures. By knowing your status, personal data, or location, foreign agencies have the ability to track and discover incriminating evidence that can be used against you. This can lead to blackmail or other unwanted situations.

Your social postings can get you deported and cause major embarrassment for the U.S. government. In January of 2014, Wayne May and his wife Alicia Muller May were effectively deported from their post at the U.S. Embassy in India. Although many speculate that this was in response to the arrest of an Indian diplomat in New York, it is clear that social media was the tool in which India justified their decision.

The Mays were your typical embassy workers. Wayne May worked in the Security Department, while Alicia May was the Community Liaison Officer. However, it wasn't their actions at work that caused them to be deported. Alicia May often posted comments about life in India. Multiple times she complained about the inability to eat meat or satirically wrote quips about hardships in India to include the poor air quality, trash, and noise pollution. However, due to their poor protection of their online presence, the Mays allowed the outside world to gain access to their seemingly harmless remarks and thus created an international incident.

The point of this story is not to argue the validity of their statements or their character but to highlight how your words or online footprint can harm your career and the mission of the U.S. Government. Therefore, it is understandable as to why the Department of State (DoS) will take actions and verify a potential FSO's online footprint and why you need to social proof your identity.

This isn't to say that you should or shouldn't have social media profiles. Even with the above dangers, I still have one and use it to communicate with family back in the states. However, this only serves to show you that you should be careful with how you use your social media profile. My use of Facebook and LinkedIn changed dramatically and is now a more professional networking tool than the "my social life" platform that it was originally intended for.

So, ensure you go through all of your social media profiles and any other platforms that you have a presence on and give them a good scrub. Look at them like an investigator or State official would and ensure they best represent you. Also, be smart about what you post, and understand there are risks to posting your personal views and any other divisive messages.

The Medical Clearance

A couple years ago, a friend of the family contacted me to ask about becoming an FSO. He was a bright kid who had just graduated from a top university with a degree in political science. Well poised and showing many of the qualities you would expect in a young potential, I took him on. Over a series of coffee meetings, I explained the process to him and gave him tips along the way.

As expected, the young man did extremely well and made it through the FSOT, and QEP with ease. However, when he did his medical screening, things took a turn for the worse. During his medical interview, the doctor informed him that he was diabetic. This was no surprise to the young man since he had been diagnosed at a very young age. However, when the doctor informed him that he would not be medically qualified, he was shocked. In what most people consider the easiest exam in the process, this young man had failed. He therefore was not able to be placed in the FSO registry and had to move on to another dream.

Let me add and stress that just because you are diabetic, it does not necessarily mean you will fail. In the case above, the young man had a severe case and had some complications because of it. The point is, he had just figured it was a common illness in America and it had never stopped him from getting a job anywhere else.

Although I would like to say that preparing for the FSO selection process is never a waste, this young man would have saved himself a lot of time and headaches if he had just looked at the medical process a little more carefully and had realized from the onset that he would not pass because of his preexisting condition.

This was also a lesson learned for me as a mentor. It is for this very reason that I started this book with Medical and Security instead of the usual FSOT. Suffice it to say, I am very sensitive to this now because of the above story.

While this may sound like a story of a rare situation, I assure you, it isn't. More people fail the medical portion of the selection process than you think. I understand why the State Department saves this step for last, considering the cost and effort to perform such a check, but it does not mean that it is any less important. It is not a foregone conclusion that you will pass the medical qualification. You have to understand that the U.S. needs assurance that you are in such great medical shape that they can send you anywhere in the world and you will not be dependent on first-world medical support like provision of insulin or other types of continuous care.

Conditions to think about

To assist you in figuring out whether or not you have a good chance of passing, here are some points to think about. If in the end you are unsure, there is nothing stopping you from downloading the medical forms and doing a medical screening prior to the test. If you live within 50 miles of DC, then you will have to have your medical check done by a FSO doctor. However, if you live outside of that 50-mile radius, then your own personal doctor can administer the clearance check using the FSO medical checklist. Just let that sink in for a second…

So, if you know who that doctor will be, then you can easy visit them with a copy of the medical check and have them go through and see if there is anything they would mark you down for. If there is something, then you can talk to him or her about how you can get cleared.

But to give you a better understanding of how strict this is, here are some questions to ask yourself:

a. Do you have a malady that would require you to receive constant medical attention?
b. Are you dependent on any type of prescription drug?
c. Are you dependent on an uncommon drug that couldn't be found in places like Africa?
d. Do you have asthma, diabetes, or any other common but limiting maladies?
e. Is there anything in your medical record that could preclude you from being posted in remote areas?

Ways to improve the process

Some of the above are things you can't do anything about. However, here are a couple of recommendations that you should really think about before and during the process:

1. If you have something in your medical record that can honestly be cleared, see your doctor and have them make note that the malady is no longer there. Personally, I have a form of dyslexia. Luckily, my mother, who was a nurse when I was a child, got me the necessary attention, and I no longer show any signs of it. Knowing this was on my record, I got the doctor to see me and make a record that I no longer show signs of dyslexia and that it was a childhood issue that had self-corrected. This allowed me to legally not mark dyslexia on my application and my personal doctor agreed.

2. Do not be over-sensitive to the questionnaire sheet. There will be questions like "Do you get constant headaches?" or "Do you have any joint pains?" Only answer yes if you have serious debilitating ailments in those categories. If you get severe migraines that completely stop you and you get them frequently, then answer yes. But if you get headaches from time to time, do NOT answer yes.

3. Before signing up for the FSOT, I would recommend getting a Medical Clearance form and going to the doctor first. See if they will find anything that would stop you from passing the FSO medical clearance. If they find something, check to see if there is something you can do about that. I know I already said this, but it requires repeating.

4. If you are dependent on a certain type of drug, look to see if you can take a lesser form or a more common version of the drug. Although I am NOT a doctor, and am not sure how I feel about it, many FSOs have told me that they turned to alternative forms of medication that worked. For them, they no longer needed a prescription drug and had it annotated on their record that they were free of the drug. However, understand that even after being selected, you will have a medical screening every time you are assigned to a foreign post to ensure you are still fit for the condition of that post. So, quick fixes will not absolve you of the overall problem.

Don't forget about family medical

Another point that many FSO potentials forget is their family. It is extremely important that you apply the above questions to your family members as well.

When you receive an assignment to a foreign post, your family will need to pass a medical screening in order to go with you. If someone from your family cannot pass, then you will need to go alone and your family will stay behind. For many, this can either destroy a family or kill a career.

If you are relegated to staying in Washington D.C. because your family can't be deployed overseas or you are constantly taking foreign posts alone, your family and/or your career could be in shambles in no time.

Before you start the FSO process, take a deep look at your family members (spouse and children), and ensure they are as capable as you are to handle the rigors for foreign postings.

Sadly, after becoming a Diplomat and being deployed, my daughter generated an ailment that got her disqualified. It did not affect my career but it means that this next assignment, I might have to go without my family.

One important note to mention: When you do the medical screening for the initial FSO selection process, the passing criteria is based on the harshest conditions possible. Passing this initial medical screening means that at that time you can be deployed anywhere. When you become an FSO and receive a foreign assignment, even though you passed your initial board, you'll still need a new medical screening. However, the passing criteria will be based on that country's conditions. So, if you are going to France, then passing the medical screening will be easy because their conditions are excellent and the medical facilities are the equivalent of those in the U.S. If you are being sent to Sudan on the other hand, you'll need to have no real issues or medical dependencies in order to accept the assignment.

A Brief Recap

Now that you've been warned and you know that the first thing you'll need to do is give yourself an in-depth security and medical check before doing anything else, here's the quick recap of the eligibility requirements for taking the FSOT as listed by the State Department:

1. You must be a citizen of the United States and have a valid birth certificate, social security number, and another form of official identification (Driver's license, Military ID, etc.).
2. On the day that you submit your reservation package, you must be between the ages of twenty and fifty-nine. However, you must be twenty-one before you are selected as an FSO and you must not be older than sixty when you are selected or else your application will be disregarded and someone else will be selected.

3. You must be available for worldwide assignment, which means you must be able to pass the medical clearance—I hope you now understand what this entails.

4. Although this isn't applicable to most, if you were removed from the FSO department for any reason other than honorable, you can't reapply. Furthermore, if you were on the registry and then denied the offer to take a position, you cannot apply again no matter the reasons for your denying their offer. Be prepared to take ANY assignment they offer or suffer the complete dismissal from the registry and the program.

5. You must be able to complete a full security investigation—again, I hope you understand what this requirement actually entails.

All checked? Great! Let's move on to deciding which kind of FSO you want to become.

CAREER TRACK SELECTION

When you've determined that you're eligible to take the FSOT, it's time to choose a career track. The Department of State offers five different career tracks, some of which tend to be more popular than others. This causes some applicants to choose a career track they feel will be less competitive. Keep in mind that this career track will determine not only what your FSOT will look like (part of the knowledge test questions are based on it) but also the rest of your career in the Foreign Service. It's not possible to change your career track after you've registered for the test, so choose wisely.

The following is the official descriptions of the five career tracks with my personal opinion of each and a very informal discussion on what life looks like for each:

Management

Official Description: Management Officers are responsible for handling all embassy and consulate operations. This involves real estate oversight, human resources, security management, and budget management.

Management officers typically are: creative, fast-thinking, resourceful, and coordinating leaders.

Unofficial Candid Description: They are truly the unsung heroes of the embassy. Dealing with complaints, and having a direct effect on the embassy's happiness factor, they deal with a multitude of issues and challenges. However, with that said, they do have control on things that most people wish they could. Nice houses, best furniture, etc. ... okay, that is unfair. Having to work with housing and financial regulations on a daily basis, they always have a better understanding of the programs and are able to get more out of it.

With regard to management, think more in line with logistics and finance. If that subject and lifestyle is what you are looking for, then this would be a perfect fit. Their only real interaction with the foreign nation is establishing contracts with local businesses and the housing pool. It's rare for Management Officers to have a direct effect on the U.S./Host Nation relationship and policymaking.

Like I said, unsung heroes.

Consular

Official Description: Consular Officers help U.S. citizens who are living, traveling, or working abroad face different challenges. Some of those challenges can be adoption, business facilitation, and evacuations.

Consular Officers typically are: socially and culturally sensitive problem-solvers with strong technical skills.

Unofficial Candid Description: This can be the most exciting section and also the most ridiculous of them at the same time. Working in consular, you can be posted in even farther reaches of the world than the other sections. Not only can you work in the embassies (usually capital cities), but you will also fill the consular offices in other larger cities as well. This can be a real challenge considering there are fewer support systems for the consular offices than there are for the embassies.

Another thing you'll find with Consular Officers is that they usually have the best stories of us all. Dealing with people who will do anything to get a visa and enter the U.S., consular officers have some of the craziest tales to tell. Also, they tend to meet famous stars (sports, movies, etc.) because even the famous and rich have to show up for their visa interview.

While that may sound like fun, they are also bogged down with a lot of paperwork and have to deal with a multitude of problems at all times of the day and night. Imagine going to bed and getting a call at 3:15 a.m. because an American in your host nation was arrested or some family members in the U.S. haven't heard from a loved one in your country and want someone to investigate. These sorts of challenges are not uncommon. In some embassies, this will be the duty officer's responsibility, however, the consular officer is still the go-to person for incidents like that.

Economic

Official Description: Economic Officers help establish and maintain economic security by working with U.S. and foreign government officials, business leaders, international organizations, and opinion makers.

Economic Officers typically are: resourceful and analytical negotiators with strong research skills.

Unofficial Candid Description: This is probably the second most demanding of the jobs and also the second most competitive to get. Econ Officers are truly a diplomat and work hard to understand their host nation's economic situation while also working hard to promote U.S. companies within their region. Acting like a bridge between the two, the econ department works around the clock to provide critical reports back to state, attend functions, build rapport, and promote U.S. interests.

Econ Officers usually have the best or most interesting contacts and seem to have a better grasp on the community around them. The best Econ Officers understand local business and always know who to talk to get good deals and who really holds most of the power around the city.

Political

Official Description: Political Officers track, analyze, and influence the political climate at their foreign post as it relates to U.S. interests, negotiations, and polities.

Political Officers typically are: well-informed negotiators with strong analytical and communicative skills.

Unofficial Candid Description: This is the most challenging of all five and also the most competitive to get. Typically, the Political Officers have the highest success rate in taking a career ambassador position but also tend to have the highest burnout rate.

Always having to create detailed reports and critical analyses, Political Officers work around the clock to create products and meet with officials. Truly the definition of a diplomat, Political Officers are at the tip of the spear in U.S. negotiations and foreign relations. They also must be at the top of their game at all times of the day and even night.

It truly has the highest payoff, but in return, it also has the highest demands.

Public Diplomacy

Official Description: Public Diplomacy Officers build and promote public awareness and understanding of American values and polities abroad by maintaining close contact with key public influencers in the host country.

Public Diplomacy Officers typically are: experts in cross-cultural relations and communications with strong coordination skills.

Unofficial Candid Description: Simply put, they are the PR masters for the embassy. Using all forms of communications, they are critical in helping to promote the ongoing of the other sections as well as their own.

PD officers must have excellent writing and communication skills and must have a firm grasp on new communication platforms, such as Twitter and Facebook, while also having a strong capability of working with older forms of media like TV and newspapers.

PD officers are the sounding board of the embassy and must stay on top of the latest trends while also keeping in touch with the other sections as well.

Last thoughts on job selection

Choosing your career path should not be a quick decision. Understand that you'll need to know which one you want before you register, and that one single decision could have a dramatic effect on the rest of your career life.

I've said it before, but once you choose a career path, you cannot switch. Sometimes, in rare occasions, a Political Officer may take the posting of an Econ Officer, and every FSO must take a consular posting, but you can't decide to officially switch to a position. So, choose wisely.

Also, keep in mind that some of the positions are more competitive than others. Here is a breakdown on the typical competitiveness rankings of the position—please understand that this is an observation over the years and I have no proof of the following. From most competitive to least:

1. Political
2. Economic
3. Public Relations
4. Management
5. Consular

Political and Economics are in a tight race with both being very completive. But there is a very large gap between Econ and Public Relations.

This isn't to say you shouldn't follow your dreams of being a Political Officer if that is what you want to do. However, you should keep in mind that certain positions are harder to get, and if you are on the fence over Political or Consular, this ranking might help with that decision.

FSOT PROCESS

Registering for the FSOT

Once you've chosen your career track and you start studying for the FSOT, it's important to keep in mind that Pearson VUE, the company behind the test, only organizes it three times a year—once in February, once in June, and once in October—in different locations in the U.S. and abroad during an eight-day testing window. So if you start studying, it's best to choose one of these times as your deadline.

When you register for the test, you get to choose at which testing center you want to take it and on which date. The number of seats per testing window and test center is limited and handed out on a first-come, first-served basis, so it's best to register as soon as possible. You don't want to travel halfway across the country to take this test, do you?

Tip: If you make it through the FSOT and the QEP and are invited for the Oral Assessment, your choice of testing dates for the Oral Assessment will depend on the testing window in which you took the FSOT. So make sure to also check those dates when you register for the FSOT.

Registration for the test opens around five weeks before the testing window on the Pearson VUE website and closes again three days before. The registration form will discuss the following:

- Eligibility verification
- Biographical information
- Military experience
- Career track selection
- Undergraduate and graduate school information
- Language knowledge and skills (you will be tested for this if you pass the Oral Assessment)
- Work experience
- Other personal information

The information provided will be checked by the Board of Examiners and your information could be used in your OA, so think hard about what it is you want to highlight and be prepared. Furthermore, do not exaggerate your experience or skills, but don't minimize them either. If you do exaggerate, you'll most likely get exposed during the test process, which could negatively impact your candidacy or even get you kicked out of the process.

Lastly, I want to mention that when you register for a specific testing window, your registration is only valid for *that* window. If, for any reason, you need to cancel and want to participate in the next testing window, you'll have to register again. The good news is that canceling a registration and then reregistering offers you the chance to change your application, as you'll have to resubmit all of your documents and choose your career track again.

Taking the FSOT

After you've registered for the test, you now have a final date to prepare for. The next chapter will really zoom in on the different sections of the FSOT and how best to prepare for them, so in this section I just want to briefly touch upon some practical things you need to know about when you head in to the test center.

- Make sure you arrive at the test center early. Half an hour beforehand is recommended, as you'll need to fill out some forms and show your ID.
- Don't forget to bring a valid photo ID such as your driver's license, military ID, or passport.
- The test monitors will take your photo before you enter the test room, so comb your hair and put on some business casual clothes. Although you won't be graded on how you look, it never hurts to come across as professional considering that this picture will follow your package throughout the FSO process. This means the OA and QEP board will have access to it.
- Ensure you dress appropriately for both cold and hot testing rooms. There is nothing more distracting than freezing or sweating to death while trying to take a challenging exam.
- Bring several pens or pencils. There's no need to bring scratch paper, as a sheet of paper or a dry-erase board and marker will be provided by the test center. After finishing the test, you have to turn in all of these materials including the scratch paper.
- You are not allowed to bring food or drinks, a purse, briefcase or backpacks, electronic devices (including a calculator!), a notepad, books, or notes.
- The FSOT consists of four different sections that all have to be completed within a limited time. If you have finished a section and have time left, you can review your answers within that section. However, you **cannot review the answers you gave in previous sections** of the test.

- You will not be able to leave the room in between sections, but you do have the choice to take a break of a couple of minutes in your chair. Stretch a bit, take a deep breath, and then move on to the next part.

That was the practical side of things. Now I'll take you through what happens after you pass the FSOT before getting to the meat and potatoes of this book.

AFTER THE FSOT

Writing your Personal Narrative (PN)

If you pass the FSOT, then you'll be invited via email to submit a Personal Narrative (PN). The PN is an online form that consists of questions aiming to figure out whether or not you would be a good fit as a diplomat.

Although you will probably want to respond to each as if they are essay questions, keep in mind that **you only have 1,300 characters per question,** as that's the limit for each question. So, choose your words carefully.

You have three weeks to send in the PN (although timings may change, so be sure to check), and I do recommend you fully use those three weeks to think about your responses and craft them as well as possible.

In the next section, we will talk about the Qualifications Evaluation Panel (QEP); however, it's important to note that the QEP will look at your PN and use the following criteria to judge your responses. Ensure you exemplify the following in your answers as much as possible:

- Leadership skills
- Interpersonal skills
- Communication skills
- Management skills
- Intellectual skills
- Understanding of U.S. history/government/culture and its dealing with other cultures, as well as your specific knowledge of your career track

Here are my personal recommendations on how to structure and approach the PN section:

- Before writing your answers, start by creating a list of personal experiences that correspond to the required skills and criteria listed above. Use this list as you read the questions and find creative ways to employ these experiences as proof of your superb quality.
- When you answer the PN questions, it's important to focus on concrete examples. Don't just say that you're a good team leader, but give an example of how you've successfully led a team in the past. Focus both on your actions and the results that occurred because of your actions.

- While attempting to include as many of the six required skills as possible, ensure you do not exaggerate anything. You will need to provide references (including contact details) so that the Department of State can verify your answers, and if you make it to the Oral Assessment (OA), you will probably be asked to elaborate on some of the experiences you've listed. Any differences between your PN answer and your response on the OA will be highly looked down upon.
- Be sure to highlight any international study or work experience you have, especially in the field of international relations. This sort of information should always be a priority to cover in the responses that allow you to.
- Choose memorable facts or experiences and remember that you are competing with others. Try to make your answer stick out and personify you instead of just making you another applicant.
- Once you have completed the PN, send it to a professional editor to have them ensure all grammar, spelling, and sentence structure is perfect.
- Also, make sure to have a stranger read it. It is vital that you get that perspective because the board members will be strangers, and it is important insight to find out what impression your facts, statements, and arguments left about you.

Lastly, some practical things to consider:

- It's possible to answer a PN question, save it, and answer the next one later. You do not have to complete the PN in one go.
- There is no spellchecker built into the questionnaire, so it's best to type your answers into Word or another text tool that has a spellchecker and then copy/paste them into the PN form.
- Each answer is limited to 1,300 characters, so do a character count with spaces before copying/pasting your text. Check after copying/pasting to make sure none of your replies was cut off. The questionnaire will not tell you they cut off a sentence or two because you went over the 1,300 limit. I have seen answers where someone copied and pasted and didn't realize some of their answer was cut off, thus leaving an incomplete sentence. It wasn't well received by the QEP panel.

Finally, ensure you save all the questions and your replies in a separate document so you can review them before going to the Oral Assessment in case you pass the QEP. Like I discussed above, the FSOA will look at your PN and may structure particular questions to pry into your PN response. If they find that you have embellished or your response is different than what you wrote in the PN, this will be a negative mark on your FSOA interview.

Qualifications Evaluation Panel (QEP)

Once you've submitted you're PN, it's sent to the Qualifications Evaluation Panel (QEP) together with your FSOT scores and the data you submitted during your registration process (apart from things like your age, ethnicity, etc.). Everything is then reviewed by the panel, which consists of Foreign Service Officers who are serving in the same career track that you chose in your registration. If you selected Political, then Political Officers will review your material.

Like it was discussed above, the QEP will judge you based on your:

- Leadership skills
- Interpersonal skills
- Communication skills
- Management skills
- Intellectual skills
- Understanding of U.S. history/government/culture and its dealing with other cultures, as well as your specific knowledge of your career track

After the QEP has reviewed your file (submitted information + FSOT scores + PN), you'll be notified of their decision via email. The results of the board will not be a score, but a "pass" or "fail" remark. The purpose of the panel is to look at your qualifications and responses and decide whether or not they believe you are a good fit as a Diplomat.

I know this can be frustrating, but regardless of your results, the panel will NOT explain their findings. If you failed, you will not be given a reason for your failure.

TAKING THE ORAL ASSESSMENT (FSOA)

The FSOA consists of a group exercise, a structured interview, and a case management writing exercise to measure whether or not you can demonstrate the thirteen "dimensions" or skills that are essential for Foreign Service Officers to perform successfully.

These thirteen dimensions are:

1. A calm, positive, and alert composure
2. Cultural adaptability
3. Relevant experience and thorough motivation to join the Foreign Service
4. Information integration and analysis skills
5. Initiative and leadership skills
6. Judgment skills
7. Objectivity and integrity
8. Oral communication skills
9. Planning and organizing skills
10. Resourcefulness
11. The skill to work together with others
12. Written communication skills
13. Quantitative analysis skills

How the FSOA is Scored

When you're taking the different exercises, you'll be observed and quoted by four Foreign Service Officers from different career tracks on a scale from 1 (poor) to 7 (outstanding). Each exercise has the same weight as its individual components. Once you've completed the FSOA, your individual scores will be added up and your final average will be given. You have to obtain at least 5.25 on a scale from 1 to 7 to pass the FSOA, which means that if you fail one exercise, it's still possible to pass the FSOA if you perform well in the other two.

What to Bring With You for the FSOA

Once you've been invited to attend the FSOA, you'll be given a list of what to bring:

1. A form of identification that is either Federal or State issued
2. A U.S. passport, birth certificate, or military I.D. that proves your citizenship
3. A completed DS-7601 Spousal Release Form if you are married or engaged
4. Printout of your SF-86

5. Completed DS-4017 Statement of Interest. This document is incredibly important and you should invest the necessary time and money to perfect your response. It will play an important role in your FSOA selection process.

Before we discuss the individual aspects of the FSOA, let's discuss some general tips for the process as a whole and what you should do the day of.

- The FSOA is organized in January and in May in Washington D.C. and also in San Francisco occasionally.
- A reminder: the dates on which you can take the FSOA depend on the testing window in which you took the FSOT. You have to check the dates connected to your desired FSOT window before registering so you can make sure to be available on the FSOA dates.
  Exception: active members of the U.S. military may request unrestricted additional time to schedule the FSOA. However, when they are discharged from the military, they need to reschedule the FSOA within six months.
- Dress professionally and wear a watch so you can keep track of time during the different exercises. Phones are not allowed.
- The FSOA usually starts at 7:00 a.m. It's best to arrive at least fifteen minutes beforehand. The test can take up an entire day, and you should be available until 5:00 p.m.

Group Exercise

The Group Exercise consists of three parts: a presentation, advocacy of your project, and a debrief. To do this, you will be placed in a group of three to four other participants and be given an individual project/proposal.

The overall theme of this exercise is that the State Department or your Ambassador has four to five projects they are thinking about working on, or are interested in. However, you have limited resources. Therefore, they turn to the group of you to look at your individual project/proposal, review the information, present it to the team, and as a team, decide which projects should receive the limited resources. Please understand the objective of this is not to get your project chosen but to work as a team to figure out what is the best course of action.

However, before I get into the three phases, I want you to understand something very important:

Those in your group are NOT your competitors.

You are not competing against them for a spot, and if you all perform well, you could all pass. Treating your teammates like a competitor will quickly cause you to fail. I might reiterate this a couple of times throughout this section—hopefully you'll get it by the time this section is read.

With that, let's begin.

The Presentation

Your first assignment will be to read the information on your given project and in thirty minutes, prepare a six-minute presentation covering the cost, goals, the benefit to the US/host nation, and other useful data you can glean from the information given to you. It is highly recommended that you take notes as you read and not try to script your presentation.

Understand the requirements may be slightly different when you perform the FSOA, but ensure that you cover whatever they ask in your presentation. It would be better to have a weak presentation that follows all directions than a strong one that covers some of the instructions. I know this may sound obvious, but you'd be surprised how many people fail to do this.

Time may be left at the end of your presentation for questions. I highly recommend you allow for such. Projects are NOT to be compared or evaluated in the presentation phase. So, just stick with your information. You'll have your chance to compare and contrast in the next part.

Recommendations for the Presentation:

It is best that you go first. You may be hesitant or think that it would be beneficial to give yourself some more time to prepare while others present; however, this one simple act shows initiative. Furthermore, once you've gone, you can then pay complete attention to the other presentations, and you'll see why that is important later.

After you've been selected to go first, also suggest that you go clockwise for the next presentation. This shows leadership and initiative. See number five of the thirteen dimensions to get my point.

Follow the directions. You'd be surprised how many people miss this critical step, and in my opinion, a significant part of this portion is to see if you actually follow directions and present what is asked of you … a common theme in the FSO work life. Have I said this before? There's a reason for that.

In the presentation, you are only asked to state the data, not your opinion. Therefore, do not get off course or think you need to add something to make your presentation stronger.

Do not come up with new information based on what is in your book. Although that may seem clever, this portion of the FSOA is not about your ability to analyze but to present and follow directions.

The best presenters are the ones who act natural. When you begin, introduce yourself, and when you finish, ask if there are any questions.

When others are presenting, make sure to pay close attention. If no one asks a question, then make sure to ask one. If you notice they forgot something that was in the instructions, try to ask a question that will hopefully prod them into stating the required information. The proctors will know exactly what you are doing and give you major credit for this.

Advocate/Discussion Phase

Once all projects have been presented, you'll move into the discussion phase. In this phase, your group will be given twenty minutes to reach a consensus on project selection. Each participant will need to advocate his or her project during this time. However, by the end of the twenty minutes, a decision on which projects to support needs to be made unanimously. Understand that due to resource requirements, not all projects can be selected.

This phase is where it's extremely important that you work well with your team. The proctors are looking for two things: that your group unanimously selects certain projects within time and how you work together. Try to understand that it isn't about the conclusion but the process you took to get to that conclusion.

Recommendations for the Advocate/Discussion:

If there isn't a leader/moderator, become one. If there is, then find a supporting role and don't fight to become a leader. It's all about how you work with everyone not how you become the dominant candidate.

Designate someone to be the timekeeper and ensure they announce to the group how much time is left at the following intervals: fifteen minutes, ten minutes, five minutes, two minutes, and one minute.

Some candidates will become argumentative and destructive. Understand that this will hurt their grade, but how you respond to this affects yours.

Others may become shy and just wait for opportunities. The best thing you can do is to find ways to include them or get their opinion. If you notice someone isn't participating as much, ask them what they think. Try to get things out of them. Proctors love this because it shows that you are thinking of the team and not just of yourself.

If you do become the moderator or leader, try not to continuously be in a supportive role but ensure you present your own ideas as well. I've seen it time and time again where someone will feel it's best to show their leadership by always allowing everyone else to present their ideas and then they give the final word or the supportive/argumentative follow-up as if they are a counselor in a session. It's good to support someone's idea when presented, but don't fall into a rut of being second fiddle to the group's ideas as a whole. You need to offer your own ideas as well.

Remember, your group will not be able to support one or more of the projects. If this ends up being yours, it is best that you support it and state facts, but decline your project in sufficient time to have a set number of supported projects in the prescribed time. I've seen candidates immediately throw in the towel on their project, and this lack of advocacy hurts their grade immensely. However, don't fight it to the very end either and drag down your team. The proctors just want to see you use fact and analysis to advocate your particular project. It doesn't matter if yours is selected or not.

If it is obvious that your project is the worst, then you should present your project and advocate its positives, but around the two-minute mark, point out its faults and give support to other projects. Make it look like you took all things into consideration and made a decision that was better for the interests of the U.S.

Ensure that you take good mental notes on the projects your group has selected, and ensure you are prepared to answer questions on them and their potential weaknesses. This will become vital in the next portion.

Debriefing

Following the conclusion of your group's discussion, you will have three to four minutes to privately brief two graders on the results of the group's deliberations. One of the two graders will act as an Ambassador, and based on your debrief will ask you several follow-up questions.

Recommendations for the Debriefing

The Ambassador is going to focus on three major areas in his questioning:

1. Any missed information that the grader knows exists
2. Any weaknesses or cons that exist in your selected projects (all projects have them)
3. Embassy-level knowledge and questions that can only be answered if you know how an embassy functions.

To combat number one, you need to have a solid plan and layout on all of the selected projects. It's important that you present the facts about the project, why you chose it, the negatives, and why you believe the positives of these projects outweigh the negatives. Also, highlight how it will help the interests of the U.S.

For number two, you and your team should identify your selected project weaknesses during the analysis and be prepared to talk about them in great detail.

Later on, I'll talk about the top books that you should absolutely read if you get to the FSOA, and understanding this information will be crucial for number three. These books will help shed light on how the Embassy works together and how the different roles and positions depend on each other, plus what resources are available. I can't stress enough how important knowing this information can be for you as you go through this and other parts of the selection process.

Structured Interview

The Structured Interview is composed of three parts: Background and Motivation, Scenarios, and Past Experiences and Behavior. You will enter a room and have three to four interviewers sitting behind a table. Once you are ready, they will begin by asking you questions.

This part of the FSOA is more like a job interview. Although they use a structured grading sheet, the interviewers can ask you just about anything, like discontinuities in your Personal Statement or something about the previous portion of the FSOA.

Background and Motivation

In this portion of your interview, the questioners will ask you about background, but more importantly, why you want to be an FSO and why you chose the career path you did. These are two **extremely important questions** you need to be prepared for. Although some in the FSO community recommend you write these out beforehand

and memorize them, understand that someone sitting at that table can tell when you are reciting from memory. Instead, before you show up for the FSOA, ensure you have created detailed responses and have practiced saying these responses.

Although you should always try to be professional in your responses, understand that you need to sell your response. Saying dryly that you want to be an FSO is not as strong as showing emotion and passion in your response.

Scenarios

In this part, they will place you in a difficult scenario and ask you questions to decipher how you think and would respond. These scenarios could be something like "You are the Econ officer and a bomb blast occurs just outside the wall of the compound," or something like that.

The best way to prepare for this section is to ensure you understand how an embassy works. The more information you know, the better you can respond to the question. It would show lack of knowledge if you were to respond to the above question by saying you would have the military engage, considering that you are the Econ Officer and not the Regional Security Officer (RSO).

However, keep in mind that even if you aren't the RSO for this scenario, there are things you can do and questions you should ask like:

- What time of the day is it?
- Who is still at the embassy? Is the Ambassador there or the RSO?

You should also think of your immediate security such as:

- Am I working on secret material and how do I secure it in case there is a breach?
- Get down and cover up in case there is another bomb blast.
- What are the emergency action plans for this?

Another key part to this is thinking out loud. The interviewers want to know what your thought process is like and how you came to your conclusion, not just the conclusion itself.

Let's do an example. Using the example above, it has also been stated that I am the only one working in the embassy because it is late night. Here is how I would respond:

Me: First, I would get away from the windows and get down to the floor in case there was another bomb blast. I would also listen to the announcements on the intercom for more information since I know the Marines on post would be sounding the alarm and giving instructions. I would also get my cell phone and start making phone calls to the Ambassador, Deputy Chief of Missions, and the Regional Security Officer. If I have time, then I would call more. Before going anywhere though, I would make sure that all secret information is secured and that my workstation is offline. Considering that I am the Economics officer, I am probably a member of the Emergency Action Team and would immediately set that up in the designated area. Hopefully I would be able to establish communications with the Marines to get a status report and be able to contact pertinent personnel like local law enforcement and keep key personnel apprised of the situation.

Interviewer: Enemies have now scaled the wall and are flowing into the compound. Now what would you do?

Me: (Thinking out loud.) At this point, I would be thinking about protecting myself and holding out. Perhaps I could get armed from the Marine post or would start looking around for something I could use as a weapon. I would look to barricade the doors and find a hiding place so as to continue to pass information. At this point, our only hope would be the get more help since the Marines have probably been overtaken. I'd continue to call …

Interviewer: The phone line has been cut.

Me: Then I would continue to use the cell phone that I grabbed.

Interviewer: You're in the basement and have no cell reception.

Me: I would try to get a hold of a radio from the Marine post.

Interviewer: There are none.

Me: (Candidly.) Then I would make a mental note of that and inform the RSO later that he has some deficiencies. If that's the case, then I would jump on a computer and establish comms through email and even social media such as Facebook messenger if I had to.

Interviewer: The power is out.

Me: Is there a backup diesel generator on this post?

Interviewer: It's been destroyed.

Me: Hmmm ... so I have no cell reception, no phone line, no power, and no radios. Another option would be to move to a different location so as to establish better cell reception.

Interviewer: Can't. You've been pinned down.

Me: Then I would write notes so that people could find them later and have an idea of what occurred. I would also take a defensive position ...

Interviewer: That's enough.

Notice that at no point did I ever give up. It was the intention of the Interviewer to remove all of my options and see what I would do. No matter what I said, there would be a complication. Was what I said perfect? No. But notice I kept thinking and moving.

Armed with a strong knowledge of the interworking within the embassy, I was able to weave a pretty good response, and even when things looked its bleakest, I continued to find some way that I could be of use. Never give up and never stop thinking out loud. Make the interviewer say, "That's enough," and change the subject.

Past Experiences and Behavior

In this section, the interviewers are going to ask you questions about your past and your experiences. This is where the thirteen dimensions are critical. It's not about your experiences but how your responses prove that you exude the thirteen dimensions.

Therefore, to pass this section, you need to relate every one of your experiences and answers to something that proves one or more of the thirteen dimensions—just don't be too obvious with this tactic. To best accomplish this, prior to going to the FSOA, you should think of all the top experiences and past events and associate them with a listed dimension. Then practice responding incorporating pertinent meaning to each event and associating it with a core dimension.

For example:

Interviewer: According to your Personal Statement, you've traveled to a lot of countries. What made you want to do this?

Me: When I was younger, my grandfather used to tell me about all the places he traveled to when he fought in WWII. He used to point out how different each place was and how it was a shame he had to see it in that particular circumstance. Therefore, when I was in high school, I made it a point to ensure I wouldn't wait to see the world (Number five—

Initiative). So, I started setting aside twenty-five percent of my dishwashing paycheck for travels ensuring I would have enough to see Europe by the time I graduated (Number nine—Resourcefulness). To afford such a trip at a young age, I had to plan everything out and got creative by using hostels instead of hotels and relying on the cultural food, which was much cheaper (Number two—Adaptability). It was at this venture that I realized my grandfather was right, and from that point on, I knew that I didn't want to be a frog in a well but wanted to understand the world around me. So, I've planned a trip just about every year so as to reach the farthest areas and enjoy the different cultures.

Notice that a simple question on travel turned into an opportunity to show at least three dimensions. I wouldn't have naturally come up with that on the spot. But having already associated certain experiences with particular opportunities to show different dimensions, I was ready and subsequently accomplished the task.

The key is preparation.

Case Management

The Case Management portion of the FSOA is a ninety-minute exercise that tests your ability to quickly analyze, make hard choices, and communicate your decision. You'll be given a folder full of various materials such as memos, email communications, research, and other forms of information, will be tasked to use the information to choose the best course of action, and then write a memo to the Ambassador with your final conclusion.

To most, the Case Management portion is the toughest. In truth, I believe that only ten to twenty percent pass this section due to its time sensitivity and it's ambiguity. For most, they are caught up in the sheer amounts of data presented and do not put enough time into formulating their conclusion. For others, they are not used to the pressure and lose composure.

Regardless, you must complete the task at hand, and understand that no matter how fast of a reader you are, you will not have enough time to read all of the information. Instead, you must use what you have and present a clear argument for a particular course of action.

Recommendations for the Case Management Section

Ensure you keep track of your time. I would suggest using the first sixty minutes to do research and then use the final thirty minutes to write your memo. Many failures have occurred because the person didn't keep track of their time and had to write their two-page memo in less than five minutes.

Realize that you cannot read all the information. Instead, skim through and look for pertinent data. Most of the communications at your disposal will have a lot of "fluff." In most cases, the information you need will be in the middle.

There will be no clear or obvious choice of action. Instead, you must weigh the good with the bad and form a strong argument for one.

As you read the material, circle any pertinent data you believe will become important. Don't waste time writing it down. Later on, after you've seen a significant portion of the data, you'll know which information will be useful for your memo.

You'll quickly find that the information presented can be split into verified facts and rumors. It is best to note the rumors; however, stick with the facts when making your decision.

Concrete numerical data is always stronger in an argument than a perception or observation. Use the numbers to your benefit and strengthen your argument.

Many of the examples will have courses of actions that serve different parties. Your primary objective should be to find the best course of action that services the interests of the U.S. That may sound like an obvious recommendation; however, you'll quickly find yourself saying, "Well, that will help the host nation, which in turn helps our interests … so." No! Most of the time, there will be one that serves the interest of the United States best, and that one usually holds the best argument.

There are many resources out there to help you format a memo. But understand that you need to approach it by presenting the options, choosing one, spending a couple of paragraphs supporting your decision, and ending with a strong concrete conclusion.

Extra Resources and Recommended Practice Tips

FSOA Yahoo Group (https://groups.yahoo.com/neo/groups/fsoa/info): Here you can find others who are preparing for the FSOA, as well as read what the previous members did and observed during their FSOA. The best idea is to find people who are preparing for the same time period and create a study group. I've heard from many—wasn't around during my time—that this affords them the ability to bounce ideas off each other, practice, and combine efforts. Also, one particular page you should spend a day in is this group's files page where you will find a lot of excellent information. Just be careful though, because there is no content manager for this group, and there is some information that is misleading or old.

Skype Practice Interviews: This is more of a product of creating a study group, but doing a Skype practice run is super important. The other person can ask you questions, watch your responses and mannerisms, and help point out any issues you may display when under pressure.

One Last Tip: While the grading process is supposed to only happen during the FSOA, your assessors will also be at the test center before you start, during your breaks, and at the debriefing. Behave accordingly. You don't want them to hear you complaining about the test or criticizing another candidate. They might not admit it, or even be fully aware of it, but how they see you behave outside of the test rooms will most likely affect what they think of you and thus your overall grade.

Your Results

Unlike with the other tests, you will know if you passed the FSOA before you go home. This is a pretty stressful moment. I remember how all of us candidates were put together in a room and our assessors would call us one by one to give us the verdict. I was one of the last to be called in and was extremely nervous by the time they told me I'd passed. They all congratulated me before two of them stepped out and the remaining two started giving me information on what would follow, but I have to admit, I was too excited to properly take it all in.

Should you sit in that same room in a few months, remember that you need to stay calm and pay attention.

If you didn't pass, you'll get a private interview with two assessors and be given the opportunity to ask questions about the assessment process and future exams **but not about your own performance**.

If you do pass the FSOA, you'll receive an Immediate Conditional Offer of employment. This, however, by no means is a guarantee you'll be hired by the Foreign Service. It's merely a contract binding you to your word in case you do receive an offer to join.

Upon signing the Conditional Offer, you'll be given information on how to apply for additional language and veterans points, and they'll give you more information on the security check, the medical examination, and the final suitability review—all of which you'll have to pass before being able to actually get hired. You'll also get the opportunity to ask questions about life in the Foreign Service.

Some candidates think that what follows the FSOA is merely a formality, but it really isn't. It can take months before you receive your Security and Medical Clearance. Unless you know of some ways to shorten the process...

SELECTION BONUS POINTS

Now that you have completed the FSO selection process, your scores on the individual tests (FSOT, QEP, FSOA, etc.) will be tallied up. This total score will decipher your ranking in the Registry (something we'll discuss later). However, at this point in the process, you have an opportunity to gain extra points that could be critical to your success.

Language Bonus Points

If you are fluent in a language, you have the ability to receive points for this. However, you can only receive them for one language, even if you have knowledge of several foreign languages. Not all languages are equal, though. There is a higher need for some languages like Arabic and Chinese over others like Spanish and French. Furthermore, the better your proficiency, the more bonus points you'll get.

In order to get the necessary points, you will have to take a State Sponsored Language Test. However, the explanation that the State Department gives you can be a little confusing. So, let me clarify for you:

There are two ways in which you can get points for your Language:

1. You take a telephone interview and receive a grade of 3 or higher in the following languages and will therefore receive .17 points extra on your final score:
   http://careers.state.gov/uploads/23/86/2386f5de7f14369e5231db272ccfe423/Language-Points-2013.pdf
2. If you are proficient in Arabic, Hindi, Dari, Pashto, Farsi, Mandarin, Urdu or Korean, then you only need a 2 in the telephone interview to get the .17 points. If you would like more, then you can take the in-person test at the Foreign Service Institute in VA. If you get a 3 in speaking and a 2 in reading, then you'll receive a .38. If you receive a 2 in speaking and a 1 in reading, then you'll receive only .25 points. If you receive a score less than that, you will not receive any points…not even for the telephone interview. This is because if someone received a 2 in speaking, but can only get a 1 in speaking in person, then they most likely cheated on the phone interview.

To give you an idea of what these grades translate into, here is a candid look at their meaning and how State perceives them:

0+: Can say basic words

1: Know basic language sentences and can speak basic phrases

2: Can have normal every day conversations with some struggle

3: Can have political conversations and conduct speeches flawlessly

Veterans Preference Points

If you are a veteran and have any active duty service, you will be awarded extra points. All you need to do is show proof of veteran status such as your military records, FITREPs, etc.

SUITABILITY REVIEW PANEL

At the end of the entire FSO process, a Suitability Review Panel will have one more thorough look at your complete file to include your scores and your medical and security clearance results. Its main role is to check whether you are suitable to represent the United States as a Foreign Service Officer. It does so by checking your history for any signs of misconduct, disloyalty, irresponsibility, and/or poor judgment. **This is also where your clean social media record and scrubbed online footprint comes in handy!**

THE REGISTER

When you've passed the FSOA and the Suitability Review Panel, you'll get a spot on the Register. This is a list of all eligible FSO candidates in descending order, ranked according to their test scores, including the extra language and veteran points they might have acquired, and grouped per career track. When there are job openings in the Foreign Service, candidates are selected from the Register, starting with those candidates who rank highest.

So even when you're added to the Register, it doesn't mean you'll be offered a job as a Foreign Service Officer as the amount of candidates hired depends on the amount of people needed by the Foreign Service. On top of that, new candidates are constantly being added to the list, which means you might actually drop in ranking if candidates with higher scores are added.

A spot on the Register is only valid for eighteen months. If you haven't been hired within those eighteen months, your name will be removed, and you'll have to start the whole process over again if you still want to become an FSO.

I wish I could give you a good number to use as an indication of whether or not you will be selected based on your Register position. However, there really isn't any way to predict this. The chances of becoming an FSO at this point are solely dependent on the demand for new FSOs and the level of competition between you and the other registrants.

Just understand that it isn't uncommon for people to make it to the Registry and still not become an FSO.

FSOT & TESTING TIPS

Now that you have a good understanding of the FSO process as a whole, we're going to dive deep into one of the hardest exams you'll ever take and its four different sections:

1. Job Knowledge Test
2. English Expression Test
3. Biographical Information Test
4. Essay

For each of these sections, I'll tell you what to expect during the test and how to best prepare for them. I'll share some insights that only someone who's taken and passed the FSOT could share with you.

You need to obtain a total score of 154 or more on the Job Knowledge Test, the English Expression Test, and the Biographical Information Test to pass the multiple-choice part and be able to take the Essay. Each question in these sections will be worth one point. Understand that if you fail a particular portion, you can still pass the FSOT so long as you make it up in the other sections.

PART 1: THE JOB KNOWLEDGE TEST

Format of the test

The Job Knowledge test has sixty multiple-choice questions that need to be answered in forty minutes, with one point per question. That means the minimum score you need for the Job Knowledge Test depends on the scores you receive for the English Expression Test and the Biographical Information Test and vice versa.

What is being tested?

Your knowledge and understanding of subjects required to perform successfully as a Foreign Service Officer. These subjects are:

- U.S. Government
- U.S. History
- U.S. Society and Culture
- World History and Geography
- Economics
- Mathematics and Statistics
- Management
- Communications
- Computers

The Job Knowledge Test is an ever-evolving exam that is recreated every year. Although they keep the same format and layout, the questions change. Therefore, just because you took a previous test does not mean you will have a knowledge advantage over those who haven't.

That being said, there are a couple of trends that have been noticed that have given some test takers a slight edge over others. Pearson VUE, the test maker, has a history of focusing more on current events in their questions. So, if Russia has been in the news recently, there may be some Russian geography questions or history questions. The same goes for important events as well. Although this isn't always the case, many other FSOs have found this to be commonplace in the past.

Tips on studying and taking the Job Knowledge Test

- Take several practice tests to get a feel for the kind of questions that are being asked. By taking multiple practice tests, you'll notice that certain geographical areas, economic theories, people, etc. get more attention than others. I've prepared a practice test for you that's representative of the kind of questions you'll get on the FSOT, but I also listed the official Department of State's Practice Test in the Resources section as well as my personal recommended reading section below.

- Focus on countries that have been in the news twelve to eighteen months prior to your test date, and try to limit the amount of countries to fifteen based on the amount and importance of events that occurred there.
- Focus on important international events over the past four years.
- Pay attention to connections between countries that have been in the news and the U.S.
- Pay attention to historical events and facts that make countries unique (for example, the Inca culture in Peru as compared to the Mayan culture in Mexico and Central America). The test will not focus on the mundane but more importantly focus on things that well-traveled and cultured people would know. I call this "Wikipedia Level" knowledge, as in, knowledge you would find readily on Wikipedia by skimming it.
- Understand what you learn, don't just memorize it. The Job Knowledge Test can ask you to compare, for example, a recent event in U.S. history with a historical event or ask you questions about which person wrote which book. You may not know all the individual books, but knowing what that person stood for or represented, you should be able to figure out which one is in line with their theme.
- Quiz yourself! Plenty of websites allow you to test your history and geography knowledge, among many other things. I've listed some in the Resources section of this book as well as in the recommended reading section.
- Refresh how to do math on a piece of paper and how to do calculations in your head. Practice with everyday things like calculating the odds during sports matches or what tip you need to give when paying for your lunch. I'm not inferring that the math questions are hard. However, it's probably been a while since you were forced to do calculations without the use of a calculator or your smartphone. Therefore, most candidates struggle because they take too much time to figure out how to calculate and thus end up falling behind or they spend too much time checking their work and second-guessing their method.
- When doing the math section, understand that time is of the essence. Many candidates get stuck because they spend much of their time calculating an answer to its fullest and then checking their calculation. However, keep track of the options and when your calculation is nearing a particular option or has proven that the others won't work, choose it and move on. Calculating out the

nearest decimal will do you no good when only one option is left at that point if you mental math.

- You will have about forty seconds per question, so you need to respond quickly. If you don't know the answer to a question, immediately try eliminating the wrong options first. If you're still not sure, simply guess and flag the question. When you've answered all other questions, you can easily go back to only those questions you've flagged. If you don't flag questions, you'll have to use the "next" and "previous" buttons and go through all of the questions again to find your guessed answers. That takes much longer to do.

- No points are deducted for wrong answers; so if you don't know the answer, guess.

PART 2: ENGLISH EXPRESSION USAGE TEST

Format of the test

The English Expression Usage test has sixty-five multiple-choice questions that need to be answered in fifty minutes, with one point per question.

What is being tested?

Your knowledge of correct English grammar, word usage, spelling, punctuation, and text organization. In all honestly, this portion of the test is the most controllable, and in most cases, the most overlooked portion.

There are only so many grammar rules out there as compared to the Knowledge portion, which has an infinite amount of facts to choose from. Therefore, it can be assumed that if you put in the time to actually learn all of the rules and the exceptions of the rules, you can ace this section.

The problem is that many candidates don't think this way. Instead, they look at the English Expression portion as something that only needs a refresher. They focus on basic rules and feel comfortable with it because it's their native language and many pride themselves on their written prowess.

The English Expression portion doesn't ask the obvious. Instead, it challenges people by giving them options that would be confusing, even to a well-educated English speaker. Those that do well on this portion understand the rules, inside and out, and are fully apprised of the exceptions to the rules and when they apply.

Don't make the same mistake that many others make, and overlook what can be easy points. Take the time to fully understand the rules and when they don't apply. Get practice breaking down sentences and restructuring parts to meet the finite English rules.

Tips on studying and taking the English Expression Test

- Take a few online practice tests. If you score well on them, I wouldn't worry about this part of the test and would spend my time elsewhere. If you don't, I'm afraid you'll need to brush up on your English by using the material provided in the Recommended Reading section of this book.
- Try to stay calm during the test. If you're hesitant about the correct answer, go for what sounds most natural to you.

- Ensure you fully understand the grammar rules, but also find opportunities to practice the "exceptions" to those rules. The test usually focuses on these more than anything else.
- Subscribing to the Word Girl podcast or other Grammar podcasts can be an excellent tool to get you used to hearing the rules and learn creative ways to remember them while on the move. There are other podcasts out there on the subject but the key is to ensure you choose one that gives examples.

PART 3: BIOGRAPHICAL INFORMATION TEST

Format of the test

This part consists of seventy-five multiple-choice questions to be answered in forty minutes, with the same grading system as the Job Knowledge Test and the English Expression Test.

Some questions are accompanied by a text box in which you'll be asked to write down examples linked to your answer. The text box is limited to 200 characters, but the testing software doesn't always tell you how many characters you've written already, so try to answer using bullet points to prevent getting an error when you want to move on to the next question.

The questions will be about your life, work, and previous education experiences. An example question could be: "How often in the past year have you helped someone with something you dislike? Give examples."

Your answers will be scored based on a list of things the Department of State is looking for in Foreign Service Officers. For example, it will probably get you more points if you have a lot of experience in dealing with other cultures than if you've never left your hometown, but how many more points that would be, we can only guess. The problem with discussing this area in a Study Guide is that the answer sheet for each question is very different and depends on the structure of the question.

Keep in mind that your answers could be held against you if you are found to be embellishing and/or saying false things. Furthermore, many of the questions will be very close to each other and are ways to test whether or not you answered the questions correctly.

An example of this would be if in question #4 they asked you to list how many countries you've been to besides the U.S. and then later in question #65 they ask you how many times you've been to a different nation. Can you see how there is a chance you could mess up? Hopefully, your answer to #4 and #65 aren't wildly different.

Another issue that many face in this section is the time requirement. You have just less than 2 minutes per questions. The problem that exist is that many spend more than this on particular questions because they are trying to rack their brain and think of any other examples they can list. The worse part is that there are rarely any questions that allow you to catch up without sacrificing your potential on that answer. So it is vital that you keep track of your time and move on as fast as possible.

So, be on your toes, but you'll need to quickly flow through this section.

What is being tested?

You're being tested on whether or not you display the qualities and skills that are required to be a great FSO. Some of the qualities tested are the skills to resolve conflicts, to adapt to other cultures, and to set priorities. Basically, the Biographical Information Test is there to see how well you can demonstrate the thirteen dimensions mentioned earlier in the FSOA section.

Keep the thirteen dimensions in mind as you flow through the questions and answer truthfully.

Tips on studying and taking the Biographical Information Test

- Do not think that you don't need to prepare for the Biographical Information section. Many candidates pass the Job Knowledge and the English Expression Tests but fail the Biographical Information Test.
- Make sure you know your own resume inside out. Make a list of everything you've ever done in your life, and write down how those things could apply to the test. That trip you planned for five of your friends? That shows your organizational skills and initiative! To make it easier, open an excel sheet, and create a new line for each of the thirteen dimensions. Then create a column for different phases or things in your life like college, your first job, each of your hobbies, your family, etc. Then try to come up with four instances in which you've demonstrated each dimension in each of your "life areas." Memorize those examples for the test. This way you'll already have (part of) your answers ready and will be less pressured by time. There are cases of candidates who fail the Biographical Information section simply because they didn't have enough time to answer all the questions. Remember, you only have less than two minutes per question.
- Whatever the question is, interpret it broadly. Meetings don't only take place in offices, and conflicts can just as easily occur within your sports team as in the working space.
- But don't interpret a question too broadly. If it asks you to list which books you've read recently, don't include magazine or journals. Remember that you'll have to be able to defend your answers. If you say you've led ten meetings in the last year, but you can't even list one example, you're probably in trouble. Plus, if you make it to the Oral Assessment, you'll probably be asked to elaborate on some of the answers you gave in the Biographical Information Test as well.

- Although the Department of State doesn't specify what exactly they're looking for with the Biographical Information Test, you can easily deduce some requirements when looking at what they state would make a great FSO: "proven leadership skill, relevant overseas experience, solid team-building and interpersonal skills, and a history of tenacity and achievement in difficult tasks." If you can answer positively on questions in regard to these skills and can give relevant life experience examples as well, that will greatly help your test score.

- Go get those requirements. If you happen to start studying for the FSOT months in advance, you can actually go out and "acquire" experiences that you know will do well in this section of the test. Volunteer in your community. Take some time to travel and jump from place to place. Find opportunities to bolster your credentials. You'd be surprised how one backpacking trip through Europe can really bolster a lot of your answers in this section. Just look at those thirteen dimensions again and you'll see how these simple tweaks months before the test can really set you up for success.

- Be consistent. Biographical information or personal analysis tests tend to ask the same question in a variety of ways to see whether the candidate repeats his answer or not. Don't answer "very often" to the question if friends often come to you with their problems and then answer "not many" if they ask you how many friends think you're a good listener.

- It's better to write down four examples that aren't as detailed rather than only two examples that are more detailed.

- Read the instructions carefully but quickly. You don't have a lot of time, but it would be a shame to give the wrong examples because you misread the instructions. This happens more than you think.

- Be brief. If the question is to list examples of times you took on a leading role, don't write down a whole paragraph about how you grouped five very different but bright students together to work on this science project that ... "DING! Time's up!" Just list: scouts leader, science project coordinator, football team captain, etc.

- If you get a question that asks you something that you know you might get caught up in later, then flag is so that later you can check it. For example, if it asks you to list how many times you resolved a problem for your friends, you can flag it. That way if you see the question again but asked differently, you can always refer back to the flagged question and ensure there is continuity.

PART 4: ESSAY

Format of the test

You'll be given an essay prompt introducing a subject (may be current affairs) and two or more opinions on the subject. You need to decide which opinion you'll defend in an essay of three to five paragraphs, which needs to be finished in thirty minutes.

Grades are given on a scale of 1 to 6 by two graders, and you need a total of at least 6/12 to pass. However, you'll only be graded on the essay if you've first passed the multiple-choice sections of the FSOT.

What is being tested?

The quality of the candidate's writing, and more importantly, his/her capability to develop ideas, structure thoughts in a text, use clear language, and apply standard conventions.

The opinions expressed by the candidate in the essay are not taken into account during the evaluation. It's all about your writing skills and your presentation of your argument.

Tips for preparing and writing the Essay

- Practice writing under pressure and within a time requirement. You'll only get thirty minutes, so practice writing essays in twenty-five minutes or less. That way you cover extra time you might need during the test because of stress, or you'll have a few minutes left to go over your essay again and correct any spelling mistakes you might have made.
- Practice writing within an essay structure, but keep it simple. Start with an introductory paragraph that contains a clear thesis. Follow with two or three body paragraphs that each brings an argument supporting your thesis. In each, add an opposing argument and say why it's wrong. Then end your essay with a conclusion that sums up what you wrote before.
- You will have to include one or two facts to support your thesis. This is where a strong knowledge of current events will come into play.
- Check your grammar and spelling each time you've written a practice essay. Be mindful of where you make mistakes when writing under time pressure. There will be no spellchecker on the test computer.
- Your knowledge on the topic that you need to write about isn't as important as you think, but make sure you don't deviate to another topic.

- You will get a sheet of scratch paper or a dry erase board to draft your essay, but you won't really have the time to use it. I suggest drafting a very raw outline and then focusing on the writing, as you only have thirty minutes.
- Keep it brief. It's better to write a shorter essay with no spelling mistakes because you had the time to proofread than a longer one with mistakes because you ran out of time.
- Take a clear position and don't waffle. Playing both sides of the coin does not help you in this case but will only make you fail.

FSOT RESULTS LAYOUT

After you've taken the FSOT, you'll probably be dying to find out how you did. You won't receive your test score until three to four weeks after the exam though. While waiting for that email, you should think positively and start preparing for your Qualification Evaluation Panel, as I mentioned above.

FSOT PRETEST

This section contains a pretest that will help you to discover which parts of the FSOT you are weakest in and which ones you are strong in. It's possible that you have a knack for U.S. History but are terrible at economics. The idea is that after taking this test, you will know which area to focus more of your time on and which areas you'll need to focus on the least. This way you'll be more effective and efficient in your preparations.

First, it's important to know where you stand so that you can keep this in mind while creating your study plan and tackling the material.

JOB KNOWLEDGE PRETEST

The Job Knowledge pretest will test your knowledge on a wide array of subjects. There are no time limits for this pretest, but if you'd like to simulate the real FSOT testing conditions, try to finish this Job Knowledge pretest in twenty-four minutes.

With that, let's begin ...

FSOT JOB KNOWLEDGE PRETEST

U.S. Government

1. What is the main way the U.S. government controls its money supply?

    A. Changes in interest rates
    B. Raising taxes
    C. Striving for high economic growth
    D. Regulating inflation

2. According to the constitutional principle of checks and balances, what oversight can Congress exercise in respect to the presidential power of appointment?

    A. Congress may propose constitutional amendments
    B. The Senate may reject cabinet level nominees
    C. Congress may override presidential vetoes of legislation
    D. The Senate may reject treaties signed by the president

3. Which of the following does not automatically confer U.S. citizenship?

    A. Being born in the U.S.
    B. Having one U.S. citizen as a parent
    C. Going through the nationalization process
    D. Being born in Puerto Rico

4. The Fifth through Eighth Amendments to the United States Constitution protect the individual right to which of the following?

    A. Protection from unreasonable search and seizure and quartering of soldiers in peacetime
    B. Due process in a court of law
    C. Reserved powers not specifically granted to the federal government
    D. Freedom of expression

U.S. History

5. Which of the following was an outcome of the Cuban Missile Crisis?

    A. Kennedy put nuclear missiles in Turkey.
    B. The Soviets built the Berlin Wall.
    C. Kennedy and Khrushchev began holding regular meetings.
    D. The Nuclear Test Ban Treaty was signed.

6. What did the "termination" approach to Native American relations with the Federal government argue for?

    A. The elimination of Native American reservations
    B. The end of granting Native Americans U.S. citizenship
    C. Ending recognition of Native American tribes as legal entities
    D. Ending Native American immunity to state laws

7. What act caused President Ford's popularity to plummet?

    A. His decision to raise taxes
    B. His decision to run for election to office
    C. His decision to pardon President Nixon
    D. His popularity didn't plummet; it was low throughout his tenure.

8. The Temperance movement was most concerned with which of the following?

    A. Smoking
    B. Slavery
    C. Alcohol
    D. Voting rights

U.S. Society and Culture

9. The Scopes trial in Tennessee, which captured national and international media attention in 1925, centered on what controversial issue?

   A. Organized prayer in public schools
   B. Teaching the theory of evolution in public schools
   C. Public school segregation
   D. Mandatory school attendance

10. What did Dr. Spock tell women regarding their children?

   A. To raise children with fathers as equal partners
   B. To be affectionate and trust their own instincts regarding their children
   C. To focus on meeting goals outside of the home
   D. To hire other people to help raise their children

11. In the late 19th Century, a new form of entertainment grew out of minstrel shows and became popular with American families by including dancing, singing, juggling, animals, and other acts. Which of the following best describes this form of entertainment?

   A. Burlesque
   B. Circus
   C. Revue
   D. Vaudeville

12. What role do syndicates play in the news industry?

   A. They operate chain newspapers.
   B. They control the media in certain regions.
   C. They gather and sell the work of journalists, photographers, and others en masse.
   D. They organize collective bargaining for editors.

World History and Geography

13. Since the organization's creation in 1992, which eligible nation has not joined the European Union?

     A. Switzerland
     B. Poland
     C. Slovenia
     D. Greece

14. The Strait of Gibraltar and the Suez Canal are both important for what reason?

     A. They are manmade waterways into the Mediterranean.
     B. They control trade in and out of the Mediterranean.
     C. Both were formerly British-controlled waterways.
     D. They are ideal points to launch an attack from

15. Which factor contributed to the flourishing of the Renaissance in Northern Italy?

     A. Liberal laws that promoted free expression
     B. Loyalty to the Byzantine Church
     C. The presence of democratic city-states
     D. A wealthy elite who supported the arts

16. In the Pacific War, Bolivia lost and became a land-locked country. Who defeated Bolivia and took away their access to the sea?

     A. Peru
     B. Chile
     C. Argentina
     D. Brazil

Management

17. In conducting an employee evaluation, which of the following is a "soft" area to which employees are most likely to take personal offense?

    A. Sales figures
    B. Absenteeism
    C. Teamwork
    D. Production quotas

18. Which business strategy relies on production that adjusts to meet immediate market demand to reduce the costs associated with idle workers and facilities?

    A. Industrial production
    B. Just-in-time production
    C. Last-in, first-out production
    D. Streamlined production

19. What is the main purpose of the board of directors?

    A. To represent shareholders
    B. To provide oversight for the CEO
    C. To protect their own interests
    D. To ensure that quarterly projections are met

20. When a manager is using personal involvement as a motivational strategy, the biggest risk is with those employees who:

    A. Have low self-esteem and cannot form high performance expectations
    B. Make only verbal commitments to their goals
    C. Make a public commitment as a group instead of as individuals
    D. Are overconfident in their performance abilities

Economy

21. In the United States, which industry could best be defined as an oligopoly?

    A. Shoe manufacturing
    B. Automobile manufacturing
    C. Publishing
    D. Home construction

22. Why might the market value of a software firm be higher than its book value?

    A. The market is placing value on the firm's intellectual assets.
    B. Software is often priced incorrectly.
    C. Tech firms use different accounting procedures than traditional firms.
    D. There is no reason for the market value to be higher.

23. Which of the following would not be included in the USA GDP?

    A. Government spending
    B. The salary of a non-U.S. citizen working in the U.S.
    C. Profit from a factory owned by a U.S. citizen but operated in Brazil
    D. Money spent by an Italian company in the U.S.

24. The interest rate at which the Federal Reserve lends to member banks is called:

    A. The Discount rate
    B. The Federal Funds rate
    C. The LIBOR rate
    D. The Treasury rate

Mathematics

25. If you travel to Mexico while the exchange rate from U.S. dollars to pesos is $1 = 10.85, what would be your total expenditure in U.S. dollars for two nights in a hotel at 550 pesos per night, six meals at 78 pesos each, and four cab rides at 84 pesos each?

    A. $101.38
    B. $116.31
    C. $144.52
    D. $175.48

26. If asked to provide the quotient of your division's clocked work hours (Hours) and the number of division employees (Employees), the answer would be calculated by which of the following formulas?

    A. Hours + Employees = Quotient
    B. Hours x Employees = Quotient
    C. Hours / Employees = Quotient
    D. (Hours + Employees) / Employees = Quotient

27. An employee performance appraisal system operates on a 5-point scale with a weighted average based on the following: Supervisor evaluation 50%, co-worker evaluations 10%, employee self-evaluation 20%, and performance data 20%. What is the weighted average or score for any employee's performance who receives the following scores: Supervisor – 4.5, co-workers – 4.5, self – 4.25, performance data – 3.75?

    A. 4.25
    B. 4.30
    C. 4.35
    D. 4.50

28. If simple interest is calculated using the formula A=P(1+nr) where A is total principle and interest, P is principle, n is number of years, and r is rate, what would be the simple interest earned on an investment of $2000.00 at 12.5% for 9 years?

    A. $4250.00
    B. $2250.00
    C. $1250.00
    D. $250.00

Communication

29. In order to convince your audience to support your proposed changes to the organization's structure, any speech to them must be of what type?

   A. Informative
   B. Persuasive
   C. Entertaining
   D. Impromptu

30. What is a pseudo-event?

   A. An event that is faked in front of cameras
   B. An event that is put on specifically to gain publicity
   C. An unimportant event that gets overhyped on a slow news day
   D. A re-enactment of a real event

31. During a conversation, when a friend nods at something you have said, what is this an example of?

   A. Feedback in personal communication
   B. Noise in personal communication
   C. Noise in mass communication
   D. Encoding

32. A reporter is conducting an interview on the record and recording it on tape. After 15 minutes, the source requests that the reporter turn the tape off before providing some additional information on a political candidate. After providing this information, the reporter turns the recorder back on. When writing the story, which of the following is most likely to happen:

   A. The reporter can provide quotes on what the source said during the whole interview, regardless of whether the recorder was on or off.
   B. The reporter can provide quotes on what the source said during the recorded portions of the interview but can only paraphrase the information given when the recorder was turned off.
   C. The reporter can provide quotes on what the source said during the recorded portions of the interview but cannot provide any information given while the recorder was turned off.
   D. The reporter can provide quotes of what was said while the recorder was on, but he cannot name the source when paraphrasing information during the portion that was not recorded.

Computer

33. In Microsoft Excel, what function does SUMIF perform?

    A. Addition of all cells
    B. Addition of all cells within certain specifications
    C. Addition of all cells with positive numbers
    D. Addition of all cells in one column

34. What is random about random access memory (RAM)?

    A. It begins looking for data randomly.
    B. It stores data in a random place.
    C. Its actual total capacity is somewhat random.
    D. It isn't literally random, but it can access any data point at any time.

35. What is the main disadvantage of backward compatibility?

    A. Older programs aren't as good as new ones.
    B. Old programs may run, but they often run badly.
    C. Systems that are backward compatible must be more complex.
    D. Old programs and new programs often have runtime conflicts.

36. Why is a CPU's cache important?

    A. The cache size determines the number of threads the CPU can handle.
    B. The cache size determines how many programs the CPU can interact with.
    C. Without a cache, the CPU can only hold one number at a time.
    D. Without a cache, the CPU will miss lots of clock cycles.

JOB KNOWLEDGE PRETEST ANSWER KEY

U.S. Government

1. A: The Federal Reserve System raises and lowers the prime rate to regulate the nation's money supply.

2. B. Article II, Section 2 of the U.S. Constitution grants the president the power of appointment to numerous high-ranking government positions with the approval of the Senate. This includes federal judges, ambassadors, and public ministers and consuls, which has been interpreted to include cabinet secretaries.

3. B: Having one U.S. citizen as a parent does not automatically confer U.S. citizenship. The parent must have lived in the U.S. for at least five years for his or her child to qualify for citizenship.

4. B: These amendments protect due process rights such as legal representation, speedy jury trial, reasonable bail, and no cruel or unusual punishment.

U.S. History

5. D: The Cuban Missile Crisis resulted in the signing of the Nuclear Test Ban Treaty. Both nations realized how close they had come to a nuclear confrontation and decided steps needed to be taken to ease the tension.

6. C: The termination approach would have ended recognition of Native American tribes as legal entities. Tribes still have limited sovereignty on reservations and are not subject to state law.

7. C: President Ford's decision to pardon President Nixon caused his popularity to plummet. He believed the pardon would allow America to move past Nixon's crimes instead of being dragged through a lengthy, public trial.

8. C: The temperance movement was concerned with alcoholism and with reducing (or eliminating) the consumption of alcohol. Ultimately, the 18th amendment to the Constitution prohibited alcohol consumption in the U.S.

U.S. Society and Culture

9. B: The Scopes or so-called "monkey" trial was an orchestrated attempt to force a court opinion on state statutes outlawing the teaching of evolution in public schools. The case garnered extensive media coverage featuring numerous prominent lawyers as well as the ACLU. Although the courts upheld the state law outlawing evolution instruction, that precedent would be overturned in later court decisions.

10. B: Dr. Spock told women to be affectionate and trust their own child-raising instincts. His book, *Baby and Child Care*, told women, "You know more than you think you do." This contradicted years of child-raising advice that had focused on discipline.

11. D: Vaudeville became popular with families in the late 19th Century by combining acts from musicians, acrobats, and magicians such as Harry Houdini.

12. C: Syndicates gather and sell the work of journalists, photographers, and others. The same stories written for the Associated Press, Reuters, and others can be read in newspapers around the world.

World History and Geography

13. A: Some of the factors influencing Switzerland's decision not to join to date include incompatibility with the Swiss form of direct democracy that involves numerous public initiatives and referendums, concerns about maintaining neutrality, and cost.

14. B: The Strait of Gibraltar and the Suez Canal are important because they control trade routes in and out of the Mediterranean. The Strait of Gibraltar isn't manmade and is still controlled by the British.

15. D: The presence of a wealthy elite who supported the arts contributed to the flourishing of the Renaissance in Northern Italy. The de Medici family is particularly known for supporting great artists.

16. B: The Pacific War was between Chile and the allied forces of both Bolivia and Peru from 1879-1883. When Chile won, they took a significant portion of land from both Peru and Bolivia and ended up making Bolivia a land locked country. Knowing that the name of the war is "Pacific" and understanding that in today, there are only two countries that are between Bolivia and the Pacific ocean, you would have only two options: Chile and Peru.

Management

17. C. Employees tend to respond reasonably to evaluations of black-and-white categories such as sales figures. This is an area that is difficult to dispute. Employees might be disappointed in low numbers or make excuses, but they are not likely to take personal offense to the observations. Softer areas such as communication skills, teamwork, or customer relations are less defined. Employees are more likely to take criticism in these areas personally.

18. B: This strategy is called just-in-time production. This strategy relies on highly dependable processes to cut overhead, giving the company a competitive advantage.

19. A: The main purpose of the board of directors is to represent shareholders. Shareholders own the company, and the board must act to protect their interests. As a practical matter, members of the board might also be major shareholders.

20. A: Personal involvement can build deep commitment to success and high performance standards by allowing employees a role in developing their own goals. Employees with low self-esteem need managerial support in improving their self-image to create correspondingly high goals. Verbal commitments and public group commitments have typical high success rates.

Economy

21. B: Oligopoly is defined as an industry with only a few competitors in which the actions of one impact the others such as with production, pricing, features, etc.

22. A: The market value might be higher because the market is pricing based on the firm's intellectual assets. Even if there are no major products being sold, the market might trust that a talented group of software engineers will produce a winning program soon.

23. A: Profit from a factory owned by a U.S. citizen that is operated in Brazil would not be included in the U.S. gross domestic product, though it would be included in gross national product. GDP measures productivity that happens within a country, regardless of who is responsible for it. Gross national product measures the productivity of a nation's citizens, regardless of where those citizens are operating.

24. A: The Discount rate is the rate at which the Federal Reserve lends money to banks. The Federal Funds rate is the rate at which banks lend to each other in the overnight market to meet their reserve requirements. The LIBOR rate is a rate at which banks lend to each other. The Treasury rate is a rate at which the U.S. Treasury borrows money.

Mathematics and Statistics

25. D: Add all expenditures in pesos. Divide by 10.85 to convert back to American dollars.

26. C. Quotient is the result of division of one number into another.

27. B: Weighed average would be calculated with this formula: (0.50)(4.5) + (0.10)(4.5) + (0.20)(4.25) + (0.20)(3.75) = Employee score

28. B: Apply numbers to formula to find that A=$4250.00. Subtract principle amount of $2000.00 to find simple interest earned.

Communication

29. B: While informative and entertaining speeches could serve your purpose, they are not required. After leaving a successful persuasive speech, people would want to make change. Impromptu speaking should be avoided as it lacks the key element of planning.

30. B: A pseudo-event is an event that is specifically put on to gain publicity. Pseudo-events differ from normal PR events because the organizers attempt to make the event seem natural.

31. A: This is an example of feedback in personal communication. Although the process is largely unconscious, people are constantly giving each other subtle cues about the direction of the conversation.

32. A: Unless the source requested that the interview be off the record or on background, the reporter can quote anything said during the interview, whether the recorder was on or off. The reporter can write notes while the interviewee speaks so that he can accurately quote him in the article.

Computer

33. B: SUMIF looks at all data in designated cells and adds the value of those cells that meet a specific criteria specified in the formula such as positive integers only or values that fall in a certain range only.

34. D: Random access memory can access any data point at any time. Compare this with an old 8-track, which always had to start from the beginning and play to the end, or a cassette tape, which could only play the bit of tape currently exposed.

35. C: The main disadvantage is that systems that are backward compatible are more complex. This generally makes them less stable and more vulnerable to attack from hackers. Windows strives for backward compatibility, while Apple operating systems do to a lesser degree, and many Linux distributions do not attempt to be backward compatible.

36. D: Without a cache, the CPU will miss many clock cycles. The CPU does calculations; it doesn't store memory. If data is needed to perform a calculation, then the CPU has to wait for it to arrive. Holding data in the cache minimizes the delay. The faster the CPU, the larger the cache needs to be to make full use of it.

Total score Job Knowledge Pretest: **/36**

ENGLISH EXPRESSION PRETEST

This English Expression pretest will examine your knowledge of English grammar, spelling, and word use. If you'd like to simulate the time pressure you'll be under during the FSOT for this part of the test, try to answer all questions within seven minutes.

Food and the methods of preparing dishes have been <u>always</u> (1) influenced by climate and geography. You'll find more seafood along the coasts and more livestock meat inland. Stir-fry, as a method of preparing food, supposedly originated in rural China because fuel was scarce there. Meats and vegetables were cut into small pieces so they could be <u>cooked quickly</u> (2), <u>over a small, hot fire</u>. (3)

1. The best place for the underlined word would be:

   A. where it is now
   B. before the word *preparing*
   C. before the word *been*
   D. before the word *by*

2. A. NO CHANGE
   B. cooked quickly over a small, hot fire.
   C. cooked quickly over a small, hot, fire.
   D. cooked quickly, over a small hot fire.

3. At this point, the writer is considering adding the following sentence:

   The wok is a perfect utensil for this type of cooking.

   Should the writer make this addition?

   A. Yes, because it informs the reader that woks are an ancient utensil.
   B. Yes, because it helps the reader to better understand the origins of Chinese cuisine.
   C. No, because it distracts the reader from the main focus of the paragraph.
   D. No, because it is inconsistent with the style and tone of the essay.

General food categories are linked to specific geographical regions. <u>Wheat being the prominent grain, as it is in Europe, cuisines will differ from a place where corn is the prominent grain, as it is in the Americas</u>. (4) Cuisines often vary within a country too.

Both Italy and France have a northern cuisine and a southern cuisine, for example. <u>Similarly</u> (5), there are rice regions and noodle regions in China. Spices have a strong influence on regional cuisines as well.

<u>Curry is associated with Indian food, because</u> (6) South India is the only place it grows naturally.

Food fans <u>had long debated</u> (7) how American cuisine should be defined.

Some <u>claim it's like asking, "What is American music?"</u> (8)

4. A. NO CHANGE
    B. As it is in Europe, wheat is the prominent grain, and as it is in the Americas, corn is; therefore, the cuisines are different.
    C. Wheat is the prominent grain in Europe, therefore its cuisines differ from the Americas where corn is the most prominent grain.
    D. Wheat is the prominent grain in Europe and corn is prominent in the Americas, resulting in different cuisines.

5. A. NO CHANGE
    B. In fact,
    C. Meanwhile,
    D. Thus,

6. A. NO CHANGE
    B. Curry is associated, with Indian food, because
    C. Curry is associated with Indian food because
    D. Curry is associated with Indian food because,

7. A. NO CHANGE
    B. have long debated
    C. long debated
    D. are long debating

8. A. NO CHANGE
    B. its like asking "What is American music?"
    C. it's like asking, "What is American music"?
    D. its like asking, "What is American music?"

Due to the large size of the country and the wide variety of available ingredients, American cuisine is <u>well</u> (9) defined by region. Generalizing, you could say that Northeastern cuisine highlights lobster, crabs, and chowder. The Deep South is best known for grits, fried chicken, <u>and sweet tea, the Midwest</u> (10) for sweet corn and pork chops. Pacific Northwest cuisine features smoked salmon, pan-fried trout, and huckleberry pie.

And the Southwestern part of the country <u>is famous for</u> (11) foods influenced by Mexico, like enchiladas, fajitas, tacos and chili.

<u>This doesn't represent all of American cuisine, of course.</u> (12) Some regions compete as well. Think of the competition between New York style pizza and Chicago style pizza, for example, or how, according to food purists, any Philly cheesesteak sandwich that is not made in Philadelphia, using a very specific bread, is not an authentic Philly cheesesteak.

9. A. NO CHANGE
    B. much
    C. more
    D. best

10. Which of the following alternatives to the underlined portion would NOT be acceptable?

    A. sweet tea and the Midwest
    B. sweet tea, while the Midwest is known
    C. sweet tea; the Midwest being known
    D. sweet tea; the Midwest is known

11. A. NO CHANGE
    B. absolutely adores
    C. can't get enough of
    D. celebrates my personal favorite

12. Which choice most effectively guides the reader from the preceding paragraph into this new paragraph?

    A. NO CHANGE
    B. Cuisines can even be narrowed to cities within the United States.
    C. It stands to reason that the foods people grow up eating become home cooking to them.
    D. Pizza and pasta are often considered American foods although they both have Italian origins.

It is so obvious that (13) there is no easy way to define American cuisine, which can be confusing (14).

Perhaps the best way to get to know the food of a region cuisine is to sit down for a meal and eat what the locals eat. (15)

13. A. NO CHANGE
    B. Clearly,
    C. Given all this,
    D. So obviously,

14. A. NO CHANGE
    B. which is a dilemma that can't be solved
    C. which is a problem without a clear solution
    D. OMIT the underlined portion and end the sentence with a period.

15. Suppose the writer had decided to write an essay contrasting the world's cuisines. Would this essay successfully fulfill the writer's goal?

    A. Yes, because the essay explains how European and American cuisines differ.
    B. Yes, because the essay details the differences among American regional cuisines.
    C. No, because the essay does not equally emphasize the differences in world cuisines.
    D. No, because the essay only discusses similarities among the world's cuisines.

ENGLISH EXPRESSION ANSWER KEY

Question #	Correct Answer	Hint
1	C	Modifiers should always be placed close to the word they're modifying. Adverbs can modify verbs, adjectives, or other adverbs.
2	B	Always have a reason for a comma. Coordinate adjectives before a noun take a comma, but cumulative adjectives before a noun do not.
3	C	Review the paragraph as a whole before you decide if this new detail supports the main idea of the paragraph.
4	D	Good writing uses clear and concise language. Which version of the sentence states the information most clearly and directly?
5	A	Transitions have different meanings—some show contrast, some indicate an exception, etc.—but their job is always to move the reader from one idea to the next.
6	C	This is a complex sentence made up of an independent clause and a dependent clause. What is the comma rule?
7	B	The verb tense shifts often in this passage. What is the appropriate verb tense to describe an action that began in the past and continues to this day?
8	A	Two things to check for in this item: correct apostrophe use and the placement of punctuation with the use of quotation marks.
9	D	Choose the best modifying adjective to use in this context.
10	C	Note the NOT in the stem. The correct answer demonstrates incorrect sentence structure.
11	A	A writer's tone and style should remain consistent throughout a piece of writing.
12	B	Review both what comes before and what comes after the transitional sentence to choose which option is most appropriate to the content of the paragraph.
13	B	Which option best emphasizes the writer's point without redundancy or unnecessary wordiness?
14	D	Decide what is necessary information in this sentence.
15	C	Make sure you understand the writer's stated goal and review the entire essay before you choose your answer.

Score English Expression pretest: /15

PRETEST RESULTS

After taking both sections of the pretest, you need to tally the scores and see which area you struggled with the most and which areas you did the best. However, keep in mind that the scores may be misleading. Therefore, you should take into consideration which areas you felt comfortable with regardless of the score and look at them relative to each other.

After analyzing each section, go ahead and rank the subjects from hardest to easiest. This list should help you in structuring your FSOT study plan and should be used in choosing which resources you intend to invest time with as you progress toward the official FSOT test.

STUDY TIME

Congratulations! You finished the pretest and should now have a good idea of which knowledge areas you should study up on and whether you need to practice your English skills.

Now that you know your weaknesses better, it's time to tackle them, and for that, you'll need to—indeed—study.

In this next section, I'm going to help you by providing advise on what books are required and recommended. Hopefully with your list of weaknesses and the list below, you should be able to put together a strong preparation program.

THE REAL RECOMMENDED READING LIST

No one book can provide enough information to help anyone pass the FSOT. The State Department knew this when they created the test and so created a recommended reading list for potential FSO candidates to follow.

If you were to take their recommendation and read each and every book on the reading list, you would have to:

- Read 29,579 pages
- Spend 53,242 minutes reading
- Spend $2,265.60 for all the books

I will not lie to you and tell you there is a magic bullet or a perfect short book to give you everything you need. However, if there is anything you should learn from this guide it is that when you become a Diplomat, there will never be such a thing as a magic bullet in any of our tasks. This is the life we chose.

The best thing I can do to help you prepare for the FSOT is to provide you with a more effective and efficient list of materials and recommended resources so you don't waste your time reading books and accessing material that other FSOs and I did not find useful during test preparations or even out in the field.

Furthermore, couple this list with the results of the pretest, and you should have a very targeted study plan ahead of you.

The way I would recommend you move forward is that look at the rankings of subjects from weakest to strongest based on the Pretest and use the recommended list that I am going to detail below. Then using your rankings, start prioritizing the books below, schedule out how many books you need to read per month based on your FSOT exam date, and move forward in a methodological manner.

So as to make it easier for you to find the recommended books on the market, I've provided a link to a website that has collected the working URLs to each. As you read this book, you can use this URL to quickly find the books on the market.

http://FSOTPrep.com/FSOT-Recommended-Reading-List

Also, don't forget to check your library. Although most of these books are too specialized, many books became popular enough to make it into the local libraries. If you are currently in college, then most of the books should be there.

Current Affairs: Magazines and Newspapers

Truth be told, for most of the so-called current affairs resources recommended on the list, you can get what you need from them for free without having to pay for a subscription. My favorite tactic is to like these periodicals on Facebook. By doing that, their most recent or "current" hot articles will show up on your Facebook feed. Then when something of interest comes along when you're looking at Facebook, you can click and read.

Most of the time, you'll get what you need from the Facebook posts and know what's going on from that. If not, then seeing the hot-topic post should pique your interest and drive you into some independent research when you see a topic that might be of importance but you know little about.

Furthermore, thanks to Facebook's algorithm, Reach, the more you stop and read and/or click those types of articles, the more Facebook will show it in your feed. Pretty soon, you'll see important news feeds every time you go to visit Facebook—instead of cat pictures.

Here are the Recommended Facebook pages:

- https://www.facebook.com/usnewsandworldreport/
- https://www.facebook.com/forbes
- https://www.facebook.com/newyorker/
- https://www.facebook.com/time/ – Recommend subscribing to the "brief" and getting their top twelve stories in your email periodically.
- https://www.facebook.com/wsj/
- https://www.facebook.com/TheEconomist/

In truth, I actually recommend subscribing to The Economist magazine because most of their best and important stories will not be shown for free online. However, if you do subscribe, you'll get access to the full stories online as well as their magazine. Plus, over the years, I've found them to be the most useful of the major publications.

English Usage

The two books on the official FSOT recommended reading list, *Elements of Style* and *The Chicago Manual Style*, are not very good recommendations. They are geared more toward helping in your writing and formatting but do not do a good job of following the type of English questions you will run into on the FSOT.

Instead, you need a book that focuses on the rules, creates methods in which to remember all of the rules and their caveats, and gives the reader enough examples so that they are sure they can use the information come test time.

For that, I recommend you turn to the *Blue Book of Grammar and Punctuation*. This book was almost designed with the FSOT in mind. It covers just about everything you need to know and gives you adequate practice opportunities to ensure you truly know it.

I also recommend that you just don't read through it but instead read it a couple of times, digest it, and book mark the parts you continue to struggle with.

This is one of the most important areas you can prepare for. It's a finite subject, and, if taken seriously, can get you critical points that will increase your overall score. Furthermore, you'll continue to use this knowledge as you perform in the other areas of the FSO selection process list the FSOA case management section.

United States (Culture, Foreign Policy, History, Politics)

Most potential Foreign Service Officers are usually strong in this area. Having an affinity for U.S. History and following the latest in U.S. policy, many candidates will push on to other areas and not give this the attention it needs and deserves.

I would go as far as to say that this area is the most important of the Job Knowledge section. Your understanding of U.S. Policy, History, and Politics will have a vital role in other segments of the FSO selection process and not just the FSOT. The interviewers won't ask you about the history of Genghis Khan or the works of Confucius. However, you will need a strong background in U.S. History and Policy to adequately answer most of the questions in the OA, Essays, and other opportunities.

With that said, if you were to read all the books in this section's recommended list, you would need to read about 6,638 pages and spend $230.56. So, let's make this list much more condensed and discuss a couple of other resources that will help you out more effectively and efficiently.

Books You Need for the U.S. Section

This is my list of those books, that no matter what your level is, you need to read. They are foundational and have had a major impact on my life as a Diplomat as well as having a pivotal role in passing the FSO selection process for others. Although some of these are newer, recent candidates helped to form this list so as to best prepare the modern FSO potential.

Rise to Globalism: American Foreign Policy Since 1938: Personally, I don't know an FSO who hasn't read this book. Quintessential in understanding the Policies of the U.S. and how we got there, this will be strategically important for the FSOT as well as your interviews and essays.

A People's History of the United States: There is a reason why this book has been a best seller for years. Even though I am a major U.S. History buff, I still found this extremely useful. I would even go as far to say that this is all you really need to completely cover the U.S. History portion of the FSOT.

Recommended But Not Required

The New Dictionary of Cultural Literacy: What Every American Needs to Know: An incredible book that will get anyone up to speed on the required information of pop culture. This book is highly recommended, not because it is fun—which it is, but because it is highly effective at stripping the "unnecessary" and providing information that is sure to be on the test. Furthermore, I have found that some of the information I gained in this book has been great conversational pieces while attending parties or meetings with foreign dignitaries. Once you read it, you'll know why.

World Order: There is no better person to talk about U.S. policy and international relations than Henry Kissinger. However, this book does not provide fact-driven answers as the FSOT requires but will be a foundational piece in other aspects. It therefore should be read, but it wasn't added to the "Required" reading list.

Just because a book wasn't listed above doesn't mean it isn't important. However, many are very redundant or cover a source of information that may equate to helping you answer one or two questions on the FSOT. So, only read them all if you have the time.

World History

In truth, this is the hardest section to master and my recommendation is that you don't try to master it unless you have the time. World History is truly enormous and questions can cover things like Mesopotamia to Beirut. Not only does it cover thousands of years, but it also covers all countries around the world.

To know and understand every fact in World History is impossible. Therefore, your strategy—based on time requirements—is to get a good overview of World History as a whole and work on areas you are weakest in … when you have time.

Books You Need for the World History Section

Why Nations Fail: The Origins of Power, Prosperity, and Poverty: Like *Rise to Globalism*, I haven't met an FSO who hasn't read this. It's not fact laden but serves as the glue to bind facts so as to create a better understanding of world history and how that has created the modern society or nations of today.

A History of the Twentieth Century: The Concise Edition of the Acclaimed World History: This version of the book is exactly like the name suggests in that it is very concise. It strings together an immense amount of facts but does an incredible job of presenting the general themes of the last century. I highly recommend using this as your general guide to World History and branching off based on areas you were weakest. Also, understand that this does not cover ancient history.

Recommended But Not Required

Civilization: The West and the Rest: A perfect look at the rise of the western civilization as compared to the civilizations around it, a common theme many FSOs claim they see in the test questions.

Economics

In truth, if you took Micro and Macro Economics in college and still have your textbooks, then you are set. While there are more complex ideas and theories, the difficulty level for economic questions is at the same level as an AP Econ class. Therefore, the only two books you should look into are:

Macroeconomics: Economic Growth, Fluctuations, and Policy: Focuses on the Macroeconomics subject matter. Concise and clear, it is a great source for medium-level economic understanding

Principles of Microeconomics: Solely focusing on Microeconomics, this too is a complimentary college-level textbook.

If you have a background in this subject, you might want to just get a refresher book on the two subjects like an AP guide.

Area Studies

With Area Studies, there are four areas I would recommend you focus on in preparation because of their significance today:

- China and its rise to power
- Africa and its challenges
- The EU and Europe
- The Middle East and the War on Terrorism

This isn't to say that other areas of the world aren't important. However, I can assure you that most or all of these areas will be required knowledge for some portion of the FSO process. Whether that is in the essay, OA, or whatever, you'll need to be well versed in these areas and should get the lion's share of your attention for the Area Studies section.

In each area, I'll give you two book recommendations. In most cases, the first will be the best overarching history book that also gives credit to the important geo-political issues that surround it. In the second book for that area, it will focus on current political issues and even counter-arguments to prevalent beliefs.

The Search for Modern China: This is a 900-page book that covers Chinese history starting from the Qing Dynasty to modern China of today, but for the purposes of the FSOT Area Studies, I would recommend start reading at the portion that discusses the beginning of the 20th century (about half way). If you have time later, then go back and read the rest. I can't talk about a China book without recommending a Jonathan Spence. This is a complete look at China and how they became the country they are today. While this is thick in History, you'll find that history is an extremely strong tool when answering questions about China. Furthermore, as you will see in essay questions and oral reviews, using history to back one's argument can be a very strong move.

China: Fragile Superpower: Although many do not agree with Susan Shirk's take on China's status, it is important to see the arguments that believe China will not maintain their current rate and at some point will implode under their own weight. Highly useful for just about any questions relating to China's current economic situation and how that plays into their role with the rest of the world. Furthermore, a strong argument always incorporates counterarguments and provides reason why the counterargument is wrong.

Africa: A Biography of the Continent: One of the better historical looks at the Colonialism and post-Colonialism periods of Africa that has made the continent into what it is today. In truth, it is very hard to cover a continent that was established by multiple different colonizing nations. However, from a broad stroke, this book strongly touches on the key areas of which will help you in you FSO selection process.

The Looting Machine: Warlords, Oligarchs, Corporations, Smugglers and the Theft of Africa's Wealth: Although the author is a little bold in his claims, this book serves the best current understanding of the plights that face Africa and the reality of why we may never see a rich and vibrant Africa in the future. Most questions about Africa will center on this common theme.

The End of the Euro: The Uneasy Future of the European Union: It's important to understand the mechanisms that came in to play in creating the EU and why it is on shaky grounds.

Ghost Wars: The Secret History of the CIA, Afghanistan, and Bin Laden: This Pulitzer Prize-winning book chronicles everything that happened to lead up to 9-11. It is everything you need to know about the rise of Terrorism in the Middle East and what drove us into the situation we are in today.

The Great War of Our Time: The CIA's Fight Against Terrorism: This newer book fills in where Ghost Wars left off and lends credible insight into al Qa'ida to even ISIS. However, if you are already well versed in current terrorist events, then you do not need to read this book. However, I highly recommend that you are well versed in what is currently happening in Syria.

Other Areas of the Job Knowledge Portion

This section includes Computer Applications, Public Affairs and Media, Management, and Consular. Although they are important, there really isn't any material that is absolutely worth going after and reading for these subjects with regards to the FSOT.

However, if you chose a PA, Management or Consular career path, then it would probably behoove you to read just about all of the books in those particular subjects so as to prepare you for the FSOA and ensure you write the best responses for essays and other answers. However, for the purpose of the FSOT alone, you can pass on just about all of these.

With Computer Applications, most in today's world are prepared enough for that material, and therefore, should not spend any extra time on the subject. Do you know what a CPU is or RAM? If so, then your level of knowledge is where it should be.

The books listed in Public Affairs and Media would be great reads for those who have become an FSO but would not serve to help someone in the process of preparing for the FSOT. I like to think of these as good professional development books, which would serve you best in your role as an FSO.

Personally, myself and other colleagues felt that for as much work as we put into reading those books and searching for the right answers, it ended up not being worth the time. Many of the questions had obvious answers and the ones that weren't were too difficult to answer, even after reading State's recommended reading books.

With regard to the Consular section of the reading list, I personally found this not to be worth your time as well. There are not enough questions for this section that would warrant picking any of these books and preparing for the subject at any great length, just like with the management books. Instead, I would recommend reviewing the current policies for U.S. immigration, key legal events, and understanding the pros and cons to both sides so that if you need to, you can create a good essay arguing for one over the other. The same goes for any immigration issue around the world to include Syria and others.

Extra Resources and Ideas to Help You Prepare

As it was mentioned above, you can't learn every fact in each of these categories. Instead, it is best to have a general understanding across the board. For example: you may not know when Augustus Caesar was in power, but based on your understanding, you should know that he was not in power during the time of Attila the Hun, and this will help to eliminate certain options in the answer.

But to acquire this level of understanding without picking up a book on either of the two mentioned above is difficult.

For this reason, I have a couple of resources and tricks that will help you to further your knowledge without requiring more of your time.

Documentaries

Documentaries can be a valuable resource for many, and in most cases, won't be as intrusive as adding another book to your list.

One thing that has helped many FSO potentials in the past was a simple lifestyle change. Many were able to remove movies and TV shows, and instead choose a documentary or History channel presentations. It might not sound like much, but for some people and their life-style, this simple change can easily add up to a lot of extra hours of education and test preparation.

Another aspect to documentaries that makes them a great resource is that most of them are posted online for free or on streaming services like Amazon Prime and Netflix.

One of the recommended reading books in the Department of State's list, *Guns, Germs, and Steel: the Fates of Human Societies* is a three-part documentary series and free to watch on PBS online. That right there should save you ten hours in reading and give you all the necessary information to get what you need for the FSOT with respect to that book.

The link for that particular documentary is: http://topdocumentaryfilms.com/guns-germs-and-steel/

However, just doing a simple Google search can provide you with a plethora of options on a multitude of subjects.

Audio Books

I know many FSO candidates in the past have hesitated at using audio books due to their visual nature. However, try to understand that you have almost 29,000 pages in the recommended reading list by DoS.

One way to really take advantage of this resource is to play audio books on your way to work, walk to class, workout, or any other time that you can listen to something while not interrupting your daily routine. This one simple addition to your daily routine can double the amount of information you take in while preparing for the test.

The best part about Audio books is the relative ease in which you can acquire them. Many local libraries have been investing heavily in them and you can download them by logging onto your libraries website mitigating the need to physically go in.

Furthermore, Amazon offers a free 1-month trial of their audio book service, called Audible. When you sign up for a free month, you get two free Audio books of your choice.

So, look into Audiobooks and just make that simple tweak in your routine.

AP Books

In many cases, potential FSO's will have had a strong background in a particular area. However, for some, it may have been a while since they were heavily involved in that subject.

For this type of case, I would recommend that you look into picking up an AP books like AP U.S. History, AP Economics, AP World History, etc…

These books should not be used as a method to teach you a new subject, but instead help you to remember or refresh you knowledge on key aspects of subjects you used to be very familiar with. I have seen many online resources promote AP books as their main recommendation for preparations in the FSOT, but this is a weak suggestion and has lead many to develop false securities in their capability.

Again, I only suggest this if you need a refresher.

Free Online Quizzes

Another successful strategy that others have used in the past is to do online quizzes for world history. It's not so much for the purpose of testing your knowledge but to help you find areas in World History that you didn't think to look up. In truth, many of those who I have advised said they would use these quizzes, and when they were stumped by a question, they would turn to a quick resources online (like Wikipedia—yes, I said it … but for the purposes of the FSOT, it suffices) to strengthen their understanding on the subject.

Here are some quiz websites that do a decent job:

www.SoftSchools.com (features AP World History questions which is perfect)

www.ProProfs.com

www.FactMonster.com

www.QuizFreak.com

FSOT PRACTICE TEST

So, you've taken the pretest, discovered your knowledge gaps, and brushed up on them using the Recommended Reading list. After that, you should have also gone through my inside tips on taking the FSOT.

You've done that?

All right, then you're ready to take the actual practice test.

I've put this test together in exactly the same way you'll get the actual FSOT: a Job Knowledge Test, followed by an English Expression Usage Test, a Biographical Information Test, and an Essay Exercise.

Before you start this test, I need you to do the following:

- Promise me you won't use a calculator. You won't have one at your disposal during the FSOT.
- Open the timer app on your phone or an online timer app so that you can set the same time limits the FSOT sets.
- Go to the bathroom. You'll have to take the FSOT in one sitting, so do the same for this Practice Test.
- Turn off the noise of your phone, chase everyone out of the room, and get rid of any other distractions.
- Take a notepad and pen to write down your answers for the multiple-choice questions. You can also use this as your one-sheet scratch paper for the Essay Exercise (you'll only get one at the FSOT!).
- Open a blank Word document and save it as "FSOT Practice Biographical." Here you can fill in the examples you'll be asked to provide. Don't write them on paper because you need to check your word counts afterward. Disable the spellchecker, as you won't have one at the FSOT.
- Open a blank Word document and save it as "FSOT Practice Essay." Leave the spellchecker disabled.

Ready? Let's do this.

JOB KNOWLEDGE PRACTICE TEST

Like the real one, this Job Knowledge Test consists of sixty questions you'll have to complete within forty minutes. Set your timer and try to answer every question, as you won't lose any points for guessing.

The questions are followed by the answer key so that you can immediately grade yourself.

U.S. Government

1. Where is the U.S. banking system regulated?

    A. On the local level
    B. On the state level
    C. On the federal level
    D. On both the state and the federal level

2. Which best describes the primary responsibilities of the president's chief of staff?

    A. Supervision of White House staff and management of the presidential appointment calendars and presidential access
    B. Main liaison with Joint Chiefs of Staff and military commanders
    C. Public relations and media communication as well as supervision of speechwriting
    D. Main liaison with congressional leaders and supervision of presidential appearances and fundraising events

3. The legislation commonly called No Child Left Behind ties local district performance to which of the following?

    A. Local taxing authority
    B. Federal education funds
    C. State control of education
    D. State-established standards

4. Which of the following best describes the process for choosing electors in presidential elections as established by the Constitution?

    A. Each state legislature determines the process for selecting electors from that state and is allowed the number of electors equal to that state's total representatives in Congress.
    B. The political party of the candidate who wins the most popular votes in a state chooses all electors from that state and is allowed the number of electors equal to that state's representatives in the House of Representatives.
    C. Each state's elected members of the House of Representatives serves as an elector from that state.

D. Each state conducts elections for the position of electors every four years to coincide with presidential elections, and each state is allowed the number of electors equal to that state's total representatives in Congress.

5. Which branch of the U.S. military does not report to the Secretary of Defense?

    A. The Army
    B. The Marines
    C. The Coast Guard
    D. All branches report to the Secretary of Defense.

6. In a presidential election, if none of the candidates receives more than 50% of the Electoral College votes, what happens?

    A. The candidate with the most electoral votes becomes president
    B. The Senate decides who becomes president
    C. The House of Representatives decides who becomes president, with each state having one vote
    D. Congress (both houses) decides who becomes president, with each member of each of the houses having one vote

7. Which department is responsible for monitoring U.S. borders?

    A. The Department of Defense
    B. The State Department
    C. The Department of Homeland Security
    D. The Department of the Interior

U.S. History

8. Which of the following was an outcome of the Cuban Missile Crisis?

    A. Kennedy put nuclear missiles in Turkey.
    B. The Soviets built the Berlin Wall.
    C. Kennedy and Khrushchev began holding regular meetings.
    D. The Nuclear Test Ban Treaty was signed.

9. During which president's administration were Medicare and Medicaid started?

    A. Lyndon Johnson
    B. Franklin Roosevelt
    C. Herbert Hoover
    D. Theodore Roosevelt

10. Who were the Weathermen?

    A. A group of scientists that came to prominence in the 1970s
    B. A violent, political student organization in the 1960s and 1970s
    C. A literary group associated with the Beats
    D. A folk band that included Bob Dylan

11. What potent political movement backed candidates who promised to fight against abortion rights?

    A. The Evangelical movement
    B. The moral majority
    C. The right-to-life movement
    D. Neo Cons

12. Senator Joseph McCarthy became a household name with his accusations that:

    A. Senators were taking bribes in return for rigged votes in favor of businesses.
    B. Farmers disregarded the fundamental rules of sanitation.
    C. Voter fraud was occurring throughout the southern states.
    D. The CIA was involved in many covert activities that would have been deemed illegal if they were taken through a committee hearing.
    E. Communists had infiltrated the State Department.

13. The Truman Doctrine was initiated to:

    A. A memorial erected to represent Franklin Roosevelt.
    B. Assist nations facing hostile takeovers by communist governments.
    C. Raise the price of crops due to price drops that occurred during World War II.
    D. Provide funding for American families who could not afford to build a home.

14. Which of the following did NOT contribute to the spirit of isolationism in the U.S. during the 1930s?

    A. A lack of awareness of the goals of the Nazi's Third Reich party.
    B. The costs, both in financial terms and human sacrifices, in the participation in World War I.
    C. The desire to focus concerns on recovering from the Depression rather than on strengthening the military.
    D. The discovery that American companies lobbied for the involvement in World War I and then profited heavily.

U.S. Society and Culture

15. Which African American runner won four gold medals in the 1936 Summer Olympics in Berlin, Germany?

    A. Carl Lewis
    B. Wilma Rudolph
    C. Jesse Owens
    D. Jackie Robinson

16. Which period of time in American history is commonly referred to as the Progressive Era?

    A. 1890 to 1920
    B. 1920 to 1929
    C. 1945 to 1960
    D. 1960 to 1972

17. What did the beat generation and rock & roll have in common?

    A. Both resisted 1950s conformity.
    B. Both fought for racial equality.
    C. Both movements were defined by the music they left behind.
    D. Both were intensely nationalistic.

18. Which television program holds the distinction of being the longest running news or current event program in the history of TV?

    A. 60 Minutes
    B. Meet the Press
    C. CBS Evening News
    D. Today Show

19. Who was the first African American author who published a book?

    A. Harriet Beecher Stowe
    B. Frederick Douglass
    C. Harriet Tubman
    D. Phyllis Wheatley

20. Which label is commonly used to describe people born from the mid-1960s to the mid-1980s?

    A. Generation X

    B. Generation Y

    C. Baby Boomers

    D. Greatest Generation

World History and Geography

21. Which of the following was not a similarity between Gamal Nasser and Kemal Ataturk?

    A. Both tried to modernize their nations.
    B. Both consolidated control in the hands of a single political party.
    C. Both attempted to secularize their nations.
    D. Both had strong relationships with the West.

22. The IAEA was founded in 1957, has a current membership of 140 nations, and states as one of its goals:

    A. The safeguarding of nuclear materials
    B. The eradication of human rights violations
    C. The equality of women in all aspects of society
    D. The creation of educational institutions in developing nations

23. What is the name of Gorbachev's policy of openness in the 1980s?

    A. Perestroika
    B. Collectivization
    C. Glasnost
    D. Bolshevism

24. Each of the following nations, once part of Yugoslavia, emerged as an independent country at the end of the Balkan conflict that dominated much of the 1990s, except:

    A. Slovenia
    B. Serbia
    C. Macedonia
    D. Latvia

25. What impact has the Sahara Desert had on the development of Africa?

    A. It has prevented Africa's development.
    B. It has promoted the development of alternative energy.
    C. It has caused Northern Africa and Sub-Saharan Africa to develop independently.
    D. It has enhanced agriculture throughout Africa.

26. In 1951, this country was the first country to achieve independence through the United Nations when it became a constitutional and hereditary monarchy. The country has the largest oil reserves in Africa. Which country is this?

    A. Nigeria
    B. Libya
    C. Angola
    D. Saudi Arabia

27. Bushido, the code of conduct followed by Japanese samurai, most closely parallels which other ethical system?

    A. The Ten Commandments
    B. Medieval chivalry
    C. Buddhist pacifism
    D. Enlightenment-era humanism

Economics

28. Which of the following defines the opportunity cost of production?

    A. Using a resource in one capacity in production eliminates the ability to use it in another
    B. Loss of potential profit in order to capture a larger market share
    C. Streamlining production costs to maximize profit
    D. Increasing overhead costs in order to expand production

29. Which of the following is the best example of a Pigouvian tax?

    A. A tax on cigarettes
    B. A tax rate that increases as incomes increase
    C. A value-added tax
    D. A property tax

30. In graphing supply and demand, at what point is market equilibrium achieved?

    A. When supply is slightly above demand
    B. When supply is slightly below demand
    C. When supply and demand intersect
    D. When demand is significantly above supply

31. Which famous economist is not correctly paired with his seminal work?

    A. Capital – Karl Marx
    B. The Return of Depression Era Economics – Milton Friedman
    C. The Wealth of Nations – Adam Smith
    D. The General Theory of Employment, Interest, and Money – John Maynard Keynes

32. Which of the following is true of countries that have high Gini indices?

    A. Most of the wealth is concentrated in a small segment of society.
    B. They have achieved a high degree of gender equality.
    C. They are on track to meet the UN Millennium Development Goals.
    D. They exhibit a high standard of living.

33. When the Fed enacts an expansionary monetary policy in order to increase output, a goal is to increase the monetary supply, which is usually accomplished through all of the following Fed actions except:

    A. Printing additional currency
    B. Lowering interest rates
    C. Reducing bank reserve requirements
    D. Purchasing government bonds

34. What is a liquidity trap?

    A. When a company grows slowly because it focuses too much on liquidity
    B. When apparent assets actually are a drain on the company, creating a cash flow problem
    C. When there is not enough liquidity in a system, creating instability
    D. When people with cash won't invest because they expect prices to fall

Mathematics and Statistics

35. Annual raises in your department were determined by a merit system and have been noted in the following chart. What is the approximate average salary increase in your department?

Employee	Original Salary	New Salary
John	$48,000	$52,000
Jane	$54,000	$60,000
Jim	$37,000	$47,000
Jill	$68,000	$75,000
Jeff	$78,000	$89,000

    A. 8%
    B. 10%
    C. 14%
    D. 18%

36. What is the median of the following numbers: -5, -2, 8, 12, 14, 14, 18, 21

    A. 10
    B. 13
    C. 14
    D. 26

37. You are calculating the probability that your department will make its quarterly goals. In statistical calculations, probability is shown as:

    A. A fraction
    B. Odds against
    C. A number between zero and one
    D. All of the above

38. If your organization is conducting research to investigate the role that gender plays in obesity-related health problems, out of the possible variables considered, which of the following would be considered independent?

    A. Gender
    B. Blood pressure
    C. Weight
    D. Number of annual trips to the doctor

39. The first 12% of a project has been completed at a total cost of $850,000. The project managers have calculated that the remainder of the project should be completed at a similar dollar per percentage rate. Approximately, how much should the entire project cost?

    A. $960,000
    B. $1,600,000
    C. $6,000,000
    D. $7,000,000

40. Which of the following would not be considered a digit?

    A. 0
    B. 1
    C. 9
    D. 99

41. After administering a test on computer applications to prospective employees, you consider all test results and decide to interview candidates whose scores were in the 90th percentile or higher. This would be candidates whose scores:

    A. Reflected 90% accuracy or higher
    B. Were better than 90% of the candidates tested
    C. Demonstrated exceptional proficiency in computer applications
    D. B and C

Management

42. When is an emphasis on corporate culture and intangible rewards more useful than strict rules?

    A. When work is creative and self-directed
    B. When work can be measured and evaluated exactly
    C. When a worker's output is standardized
    D. When tasks are repetitive and low-skilled

43. A company might be in violation of the provisions of Title IV of the Civil Rights Act if their hiring practices include:

    A. Requiring educational achievements that are related to job performance or business needs
    B. Conducting aptitude testing for all employment candidates
    C. Coding resumes or applications by gender or race
    D. Limiting application for some positions to degreed candidates only

44. Performance management is one method that can be substituted for:

    A. Merit pay
    B. Traditional appraisal systems
    C. Annual or quarterly bonus schedules
    D. Quota systems

45. Which of the following does not necessarily increase competition between companies?

    A. The presence of many roughly equal competitors
    B. High overhead costs
    C. Slow industry growth
    D. Industry deregulation

46. An easy and cost-effective strategy for managers to utilize in order to reduce work-related stress among employees is:

    A. Create an open layout work space where all employees can easily hear and see other employees during the work day
    B. To practice a plan-ahead strategy that minimizes the need for crisis management

C. To emphasize competition among employees by increasing performance incentives to maximize productivity
D. Providing employees with minimal responsibilities

47. Which strategy should a company employ to combat high turnover in a competitive industry?

    A. Increase recruiting efforts.
    B. Make the workplace more competitive.
    C. Spend less on HR, since most employees leave anyway.
    D. Implement employee retention programs.

48. Which of the following best measures a company's ability to meet short-term obligations?

    A. Liquidity
    B. Profitability
    C. Productivity
    D. Leverage

Communications

49. When communicating face to face, negativity is often apparent when a participant:

    A. Leans forward in his chair
    B. Crosses his legs
    C. Crosses his arms across his chest
    D. Rests his chin on his hand

50. Which of the following is an example of agenda setting?

    A. An editor's choice to put a politically embarrassing story on the front page
    B. A photographer's decision to keep some pictures over others
    C. A writer's decision to paraphrase an interview
    D. A company's decision to advertise with a given newspaper

51. When communicating information, employers will most likely be successful in capturing employee attention by:

    A. Enclosing the information in paycheck or pay stub envelopes
    B. Printing the information in a company newsletter or regular publication
    C. Presenting information at brief staff meetings
    D. Posting information on break area bulletin boards

52. Which method do polling companies use to estimate public opinion?

    A. Sampling
    B. Interpolation
    C. Trial and error
    D. Experimentation

53. Considering that some experts believe more than one-half of the emotional meaning of a message comes from non-verbal communication, an important consideration in delivering a speech to an audience is:

    A. Avoiding overdressing for the occasion
    B. Keeping your voice low to avoid the impression of yelling
    C. Choice of vocabulary
    D. Culturally significant gestures

54. What is the CNN effect?

    A. The agenda-setting power of televised media
    B. The power of media to simplify news stories
    C. The effect of the 24-hour news cycle on politics
    D. The effect of the 24-hour news cycle on other media outlets

Computer

55. Which of the following is a port used for transferring data between a computer and other external devices such as cameras and printers?

    A. USB
    B. Modem
    C. CPU
    D. Coaxial

56. In Internet advertising, CPC and CPM are most likely to refer to which of the following?

    A. Cost per one hundred clicks; Cost per one million clicks
    B. Cost per one hundred clicks; Cost per one thousand clicks
    C. Cost per click; Cost per one thousand impressions
    D. Cost per click; Cost per one million impressions

57. Which of the following processes is not controlled by the operating system?

    A. Process management
    B. Maintaining interoperability
    C. File management
    D. Memory management

58. In terms of online security, what is re-identification?

    A. Validating a user's identity before granting access to secure content
    B. Validating a user's identity throughout a secure session
    C. Requiring a user to log back in after a session has expired
    D. Determining a user's actual identity from anonymous information

59. What is a white-hat hacker?

    A. White-hat hackers are security experts who do not break the law.
    B. White-hat hackers expose security vulnerabilities so that they can be corrected.
    C. White-hat hackers are hackers who work for the government.
    D. White-hat hackers are programmers who track down cybercriminals.

60.   What role does the BIOS play?

    A.   The BIOS loads the operating system.
    B.   The BIOS mediates between the operating system and the computer.
    C.   The BIOS mediates between the operating system and the user.
    D.   The BIOS is a backup in case the operating system fails.

JOB KNOWLEDGE ANSWER KEY

U.S. Government

1. D: The U.S. banking system is one of the most regulated banking systems in the world, with regulations within each state and the federal government.

2. A: The responsibilities of the chief of staff vary with each president although these responsibilities are usually constant. This role is administrative while at the same time also serves in the capacity of personal advisor.

3. B: No Child Left Behind imposes federal standards on education nationwide. Although the federal government has no constitutional authority over education, they can distribute and withhold funds to compel state and local cooperation.

4. A: Article 2, Section 1 of the Constitution describes the process of choosing members of the Electoral College, giving each state discretion in the process and a number of electors equal to that state's senators and representatives combined.

5. C: The Coast Guard does not report to the Secretary of Defense. Although the Coast Guard is generally considered to be part of the U.S. military, the Coast Guard commandant reports to the secretary of Homeland Security and is not a member of the Joint Chiefs of Staff.

6. C: The candidate who receives the most votes in the Electoral College becomes president, only if the candidate receives more than fifty percent of the votes. If no one receives more than fifty percent of the votes, the House of Representatives elects the president, with each state having one vote. In the 1824 elections, neither candidate received fifty percent of the votes, and the election was decided in the House of Representatives. John Quincy Adams became president even though Andrew Jackson had received a greater number of Electoral College votes. This episode became known as the Corrupt Bargain after Henry Clay, the Speaker of the House, became Secretary of State under John Quincy Adams.

7. C: The Department of Homeland Security is responsible for monitoring U.S. borders. This effort involves many other agencies and departments, but DHS was specifically created to be a responsible agent capable of cutting across jurisdictional boundaries.

U.S. History

8. D: The Cuban Missile Crisis resulted in the signing of the Nuclear Test Ban Treaty. Both nations realized how close they had come to a nuclear confrontation and decided that steps needed to be taken to ease the tension.

9. A: Although many programs were introduced under Franklin Roosevelt's New Deal, the Medicaid and Medicare programs were started by Johnson.

10. B: The Weathermen were a violent, political student organization in the 1960s and 1970s. They bombed banks, the U.S. capital, the Pentagon, and the U.S. State Department, though they also gave evacuation warnings prior to the bombings.

11. C: Members of the right-to-life movement voted for candidates who opposed abortion. Although there is overlap between the right-to-life movement and the other three groups, the right-to-lifers are specifically opposed to abortion.

12. E: Senator McCarthy became well known for accusing many innocent Americans of being Communist spies. Support came from the American people due to their great fear of the Chinese Revolution and the successful detonation of an atomic bomb in the USSR.

13. C: Harry Truman believed that governments in danger of falling to communist reign must be prevented. In a speech to Congress to gain aid for Turkey and Greece, he said, "I believe it must be policy of the United States to support free peoples who are resisting attempted subjugation by armed minorities or outside pressures." This policy remained and the Cold War grew.

14. A: Hitler made little to no secret of his expansionist goals. Americans may not have been completely aware of his entire plan, but they definitely had a general idea.

U.S. History and Culture

15. C: Jesse Owens' four gold medals in Berlin were a major accomplishment for any athlete, made all the more significant given the political and racially charged atmosphere of Berlin and Hitler's growing influence. He still holds several world records in track and field.

16. A: The Progressive Era is usually marked from the late 1800s until the beginning of World War I. It was characterized by numerous reform movements including improving efficiency and honesty in government, equality (although with contradictions), social justice, and social welfare. Significant events included the passage of Prohibition and the Nineteenth Amendment guaranteeing women's suffrage.

17. A: Both movements resisted 1950s conformity. Rock & roll that sounds tame to modern ears was considered raucous in the 1950s, and the literature left behind by the beats is unmistakably hostile to the middle-class lifestyle.

18. B. Meet the Press has been running since 1947.

19. D: Phyllis Wheatley was the first African American to publish a poem book in 1773. Phyllis Wheatley was a slave who gained her freedom after the book's publication.

20. A: Generation X.

World History

21. D: Neither Nasser nor Ataturk had friendly relationships with the West. Both leaders are remembered for centralizing power and attempting to create modern nations.

22. A: The International Atomic Energy Agency was founded to address growing concerns about safety in the nuclear age. It is an independent agency often utilized by the UN in the inspections process.

23. C: Glasnost was Gorbachev's policy of openness. Glasnost is Russian for "public" and Gorbachav hoped to create a more open and free state.

24. D. Latvia is a former Soviet state, now independent since the collapse of the Soviet Union. It is located on the Baltic Sea, not in the Balkans.

25. C: The Sahara Desert has caused Northern and Sub-Saharan Africa to develop independently. Although the Sahara was not impassable before air travel, the journey was difficult and seldom attempted.

26. B: Libya was the first country to achieve independence in 1951 through the United Nations and has the largest oil reserves in Africa.

27. B: Bushido most closely parallels medieval chivalry. Both were codes of honor followed by warriors in a feudal society.

Economics

28. A: Opportunity cost might be considered the second best choice for using a resource. By using it in its primary way, this second best opportunity is lost.

29. A: A Pigouvian tax is named after Arthur Pigou, a 20th Century British economist. Pigouvian taxes are imposed on goods whose price does not reflect the true total social cost of their consumption. Typical examples include taxes on cigarettes, alcohol, or gambling. Recently there have been discussions about Pigouvian taxes on non-diet sodas and fast food.

30. C: Market equilibrium is defined as market demand equaling market supply.

31. B: *The Return of Depression Era Economics* was written by Paul Krugman not Milton Friedman. Unlike the other three economists listed, Friedman is not closely associated with a single publication. This hasn't hampered the Nobel laureate's influence.

32. A: A country with a high Gini index concentrates most of the wealth in a small segment of society. The Gini is a measure of wealth inequality. An index of one would represent perfect equality. The most equal countries in existence have Gini indices in the high teens and low twenties; the least equal have indices in the sixties. The U.S. Gini index is in the high forties.

33. A: Printing money is a responsibility reserved to the Bureau of Engraving and Printing. Except for regulated printing such as replacement, printing additional currency that is not already part of the monetary totals in the economy is strictly limited to legislative acts and oversight. All other choices are used by the Federal Reserve Bank to increase the actual cash available in the economy without changing total value.

34. D: A liquidity trap is when people who have cash won't invest because they expect prices to drop. These beliefs are often self-fulfilling because prices drop when no one is willing to buy. When there is a liquidity trap, injecting cash into the economy has no effect because people still do not want to invest.

Mathematics

35. C: Calculate individual percentage rates by subtracting old salary from new salary, dividing the difference by the old salary, and dividing by 100. Add all percentage rates together and divide by 5.

36. B: The median is 13 (the middle value). Because there are an even number of values, we take the two middle values (12 and 14) and average them, getting 13. The mean (or average) is 10. The mode is 14. The range is 26.

37. D: Probability is traditionally shown as a number between 0 and 1. For example, when tossing a coin, the probability of heads and tails are equal at 0.5. However, it can also be shown as odds against or as a fraction.

38. A: Independent variables are those that are manipulated in research or those variables used to assign subjects to experimental groups. Dependent variables are those that are simply measured or recorded.

39. D: Total cost = 850,000/0.12 which equals 7,083,333.

40. D: Digits are only 0, 1, 2, 3, 4, 5, 6, 7, 8, 9.

41. B: Percentile ranking indicates the percentage of scores that ranking is above. A 90th percentile ranking means that score was higher than 90% of scores. This alone cannot be construed as proficient since it is only a measure of comparison, not a measure of performance to standards.

Management

42. A: An emphasis on corporate culture and intangible rewards is useful when work is creative and self-directed. In these situations, it is not clear how rules and strict evaluations would be designed in the first place, and poorly developed rules would actually impede productivity.

43. C: Coding or organizing candidates by race, gender, national origin, religion, or any other protected category could be construed as supporting discriminatory practices in hiring.

44. B: Performance management can replace traditional employee appraisal systems and focuses on the whole employee picture from new hire to exit interviews.

45. D: Industry deregulation does not necessarily increase competition between companies; it depends on the specific regulations being removed. The presence of many competitors and slow industry growth both force companies to steal clients from each other in order to maintain steady growth. While high overhead costs make it difficult for new competitors to enter the market, it also makes it impossible to slow production during slow times, so existing companies must perform or go out of business entirely.

46. B: Living in crisis management mode is very stressful for everyone in the workplace. Open layouts can be noisy and distracting to completing tasks; minimal responsibility can make employees feel insecure in their jobs; and excessive competition increases stress.

47. D: The company should implement employee retention programs. High turnover makes it difficult to implement larger strategies because the team is constantly being patched back together. Employee retention programs can include aspects such as health benefits, workplace perks, vested stock options, or retirement plans.

48. A: A company's ability to meet short-term obligations is best measured by its liquidity. Liquidity measures a company's cash on hand and assets that can be quickly converted to cash at or near full value. Profitable companies with many assets that lack liquidity can usually finance short-term obligations with other loans.

Communications

49. C: Arm crossing suggests a barrier while resting a chin on a hand or crossing legs is seen as contemplation and leaning forward indicates interest.

50. A: An editor's choice to put a politically embarrassing story on the front page is an example of agenda setting. Proponents of the agenda-setting theory of media argue that media do not tell people what to think, but rather what to think about. Guiding the conversation in this way is also powerful.

51. C: Based on surveys and research, it is difficult to substitute for face-to-face communication. Employees are more interested in the money than the paperwork attached, and this form of communication is often more of a nuisance than a benefit. Unattended bulletin boards can become cluttered and out of date. Written publications are not as cost and time effective as emails and are easily overlooked or ignored.

52. A: Polling companies use sampling to estimate public opinion. If the sample that answers the poll accurately reflects the larger population, then the poll will be accurate. Choosing a sample is one of the biggest challenges facing a polling company.

53. D: Gestures mean different things among different cultures and consideration should be given to the makeup of the audience to avoid offending them. Dressing well no matter the audience or occasion is a sign of respect. A low voice is likely to prevent some audience members from hearing and choice of vocabulary is not non-verbal.

54. A: The CNN effect is the agenda-setting power of televised media. Madeline Albright coined this term specifically in regards to how CNN had affected foreign policy decisions by influencing the public emotional reaction.

Computers

55. A: USB stands for Universal Serial Bus and is the most commonly used connection method between computers and external devices. Most modern computers have several of these ports and the majority of digital devices are available with compatible connectors.

56. C: CPC: Cost per click CPM: Cost per one thousand impressions (M is 1,000 in Roman numerals)

57. B: The CPU is not responsible for maintaining interoperability; that is the job of software developers. The operating system manages system resources and allows applications to interact with hardware.

58. D: Re-identification is the process of determining a user's actual identity from anonymous information. If the information has value, for marketing agencies for instance, determining its originator allows the data to be sold.

59. B: White-hat hackers expose security vulnerabilities so that they can be fixed. These activities are sometimes, though not necessarily, illegal or controversial. Black-hat hackers exploit security vulnerabilities for personal gain.

60. A: The basic input/output system (BIOS) loads the operating system. It turns on the computer's hardware and then runs a piece of code called the boot sector, which boots the operating system.

ENGLISH EXPRESSION USAGE TEST

You have fifty minutes to answer sixty-five multiple-choice questions about the following text. When you're ready, check the answer key and grade yourself.

Passage 1: Vacation at the cabin

Like hundreds of other families here in Finland, my family stays two weeks at my <u>grandparents</u> (1) small lake cabin every July.

The members of my immediate <u>family—two parents, four children, one dog</u> (2) always look forward to this trip with varying levels of excitement. My oldest brother, not an outdoorsy type of person, finds the weeks we spend by the lake highly unpleasant.

Once there, he constantly complains that he's hot, allergic, itchy, and <u>boring</u> (3).

He just hangs there on a deck chair most days, complaining. My sister, <u>conversely</u> (4), readies her fishing paraphernalia a month in advance, and gathers <u>a medley of nets and an assortment of containers</u> (5) capture and imprison the insects that she wants to gather.

1. A. NO CHANGE
    B. grandparent's
    C. grandparents'
    D. grandparents's

2. A. NO CHANGE
    B. family; two parents, four children, one dog,
    C. family: two parents, four children, one dog
    D. family—two parents, four children, one dog—

3. A. NO CHANGE
    B. bored
    C. boredom
    D. is bored

4. Which of the following alternatives to the underlined portion would be LEAST acceptable?

    A. in contrast
    B. consequently
    C. however
    D. on the other hand

5. A. NO CHANGE
    B. a medley and assortment of nets and containers
    C. an assortment of nets and an assortment of containers
    D. an assortment of nets and containers

For her, <u>these two weeks are</u> (6) practice for her future career in biology. Dara, the dog, always ventures out with her.

Dad always has a project to work on when we go to the lake. This July, he's painting the windows again, but he only works in the mornings, so <u>they</u> (7) can go hiking or swimming in the afternoons. Mom looks forward to this lake vacation the most, I think. She is nostalgic about returning to our cabin, <u>which I can understand</u> (8) Her favorite thing about this place are the many flowers that her grandfather once planted.

The rest of the year, when we're <u>not at the lake</u> (9), we live a busy life in a noisy city. I love that it's calm at the lake and serene. I spend most of my time there sitting by the water, dreaming.

My absolute favorite time of the day is around sunrise. <u>All silent, save</u> (10) for the singing of birds.

<u>In the morning sun filters</u> (11) through the leaves of the trees <u>that surround our cabin</u> (12), dappling the earth with light. I always go outside before the sun has fully risen into the sky and jog down the path to the lake.

6. A. NO CHANGE
    B. this two weeks are
    C. these two weeks is
    D. this two weeks were

7. A. NO CHANGE
    B. he and she
    C. he and Mom
    D. the two of them

8. Given that all of the choices are true, which one provides the most relevant information

    A. NO CHANGE
    B. which is interesting because she's not a very nostalgic person
    C. a place she frequently visited as a child
    D. which has stood in these woods for over fifty years

9. A. NO CHANGE
    B. from September through August
    C. when we're not on vacation
    D. OMIT the underlined portion

10. A. NO CHANGE
    B. All is silent, save
    C. Silent, except
    D. Silently,

11. A. NO CHANGE
    B. In the morning sun, filters
    C. In the morning, sun filters
    D. In the morning sun filters,

12. The best place for the underlined portion would be:

If I'm early and quick enough, I'll get there before the fog lifts. I love to watch it dissipate as the sun strengthens, the far shore slowly comes (13) into focus as the gray curtain evaporates.

A. where it is now
B. after the word leaves
C. after the word earth
D. after the word light (ending the sentence with a period)

13. A. NO CHANGE
    B. strengthens, the far shore slowly coming
    C. strengthens the far shore, slowly comes
    D. strengthens, and the far shore slowly coming

By the time I can distinguish (14) the red canoe on the other side, I'm ravenous and run back to the cabin for breakfast. (15)

14. A. NO CHANGE
    B. distinguished
    C. could distinguish
    D. had distinguished

15. Which of the following sentences, if inserted here, would best conclude the narrative?

    A. After breakfast, we're all going on a hike around the lake.
    B. On the way, I see my brother and Zeus sniffing through the trees.
    C. Mom most likely has my favorite fresh blueberry muffins waiting for me.
    D. Even in August, it's a little brisk in the early mornings near the lake.

Passage 2: The Trail of Tears

In the early 1800s, the Cherokee people were a flourishing tribe in the southeastern United States. With a long history in the region, they had built a life centered on agriculture, family, and education. They weren't averse to European customs and lived (16) in houses grouped together in small villages or standing alone and serving as farms. While they believed the land belonged to no individual, many Cherokee owned, and (17) were responsible for their own houses and livestock. (18)

They were a flourishing and peaceful people.

They were an independent people. (19)

16. A. NO CHANGE
     B. had lived
     C. had been living
     D. are living

17. A. NO CHANGE
     B. owned, were
     C. owned and were
     D. owned; and were

18. At this point, the writer is considering adding the following true statement:

     Many wore Western style clothing.

     Should the writer make this addition here?

     A. Yes, because it supports the assertion that the Cherokee were assimilated and settled.
     B. Yes, because it provides a contrast to the previous examples of how the Cherokee lived.
     C. No, because it is unrelated to the focus of the paragraph.
     D. No, because it contradicts information preceding it.

19. Which change most effectively guides the reader from the preceding paragraph to this new paragraph?

     A. NO CHANGE
     B. They were also an independent people.
     C. For example, they were an independent people.
     D. They were, on the other hand, an independent people.

In 1827, they declared themselves the Cherokee Nation and created their own constitution. Similar to the U.S. Constitution, it created three branches of government, provided for an elected leader, instituted a council of advisors, and had established (20) a code of law.

20. A. NO CHANGE
    B. created three branches of government, provided for an elected leader, instituted a council of advisors, and established
    C. had created three branches of government, provided for an elected leader, instituted a council of advisors, and established
    D. will create three branches of government, provide for an elected leader, institute a council of advisors, and establish

Sequoya a silversmith from Georgia (21) invented a system for writing the Cherokee language.

21. A. NO CHANGE
    B. ; a silversmith from Georgia,
    C. , a silversmith from Georgia,
    D. , a silversmith from Georgia

He devised a syllabary, which created individual symbols to represent each individual syllable of a word. (22)

22. A. NO CHANGE
    B. created symbols to represent every individual syllable of a word.
    C. created individual symbols to represent individual syllables of a word.
    D. created symbols to represent each syllable of a word.

If someone who could speak Cherokee learned the symbols, he could also read and write it. Literacy rates shot up. (23)

23. Given that all are true, which of the following additions to the preceding sentence (replacing the period with a comma) would be most relevant?

    A. and books began to be translated into the Cherokee language.
    B. and the giant sequoia trees in the West were named after Sequoya.
    C. and the Cherokee Nation became a nation state in 1827.
    D. and the 1835 census found a large increase in the Cherokee population.

The federal government began to encroach on Cherokee land <u>because</u> (24) a lot of states did not want independent nations within their state boundaries.

The government set aside land west of the <u>Mississippi. And encouraged</u> (25) the Cherokee to move voluntarily. Some Cherokee groups signed treaties with the government, but these treaties were not authorized by elected leaders, and many Cherokee didn't want to honor them. Authorized in 1830, the Indian Removal Act <u>granted President Andrew Jackson</u> (26) the power to arbitrate the treaties and to deploy the military to enforce them.

Some Cherokee tried to prevent their removal with legal actions and even appealed to the Supreme Court, <u>which</u> (27) offered a favorable opinion, but the officials simply ignored this opinion.

Finally, in 1838, between 14,000 and 20,000 Cherokee were <u>persuasively</u> (28) removed from their homes and forced to move over 2,000 miles away to the area that is now Oklahoma.

This six-month march <u>becomes known</u> (29) as The Trail of Tears because almost a quarter of the Cherokee who were forced to move died along the way.

24. Which of the following alternatives to the underlined portion would NOT be correct?

   A. since
   B. as
   C. while
   D. given that

25. A. NO CHANGE
   B. Mississippi. It encouraged
   C. Mississippi and who encouraged
   D. Mississippi and encouraged

26. A. NO CHANGE
   B. President Andrew Jackson had been granted
   C. granting President Andrew Jackson
   D. the granting to President Andrew Jackson of

27. A. NO CHANGE
   B. that
   C. who
   D. whom

28. A. NO CHANGE
   B. forcibly
   C. peacefully
   D. credibly

29. Which of the following alternatives to the underlined portion would NOT be correct?

   A. became known
   B. had become known
   C. has become known
   D. came to be known

Question 30 asks about the passage as a whole.

30. Suppose the writer's goal had been to write an informative essay about events leading up to The Trail of Tears. Would this essay accomplish that goal?

   A. No, because the writer doesn't explain why the Trail of Tears occurred.
   B. No, because the writer only describes the history of the Cherokee Nation.
   C. Yes, because the writer traces the chronology of events that led to the Cherokee being removed from their land.
   D. Yes, because the writer appeals to the reader's emotions when describing what the Cherokee endured.

Passage 3: The National Mall

What is known today as the National Mall in <u>Washington, D.C., the</u> (31) result of over 200 years of efforts to create a public space in our nation's capital.

The grand idea behind the National Mall was to create a large grass area with trees, memorials, and monuments on <u>an intersecting grid, around</u> (32) the Capitol Building and the White House.

<u>Today, the main part</u> (33) of the National Mall spans two miles from the Capitol Building to the Lincoln Memorial and the Potomac River.

The Lincoln Memorial is huge: 119 feet in width and almost 100 feet tall. It shows a seated President Lincoln amid 36 fluted columns. (34)

31. A. NO CHANGE
    B. Washington, D.C., has been
    C. Washington, D.C., which is
    D. Washington, D.C., is

32. A. NO CHANGE
    B. an intersecting grid around
    C. an intersecting, grid around,
    D. an intersecting grid, around,

33. A. NO CHANGE
    B. At present, the major component
    C. In modern times, the most important part
    D. In contrast, today on the Mall, the principal portion

34. At this point, the writer is considering adding the following sentence:

    The Lincoln Memorial is where Martin Luther King, Jr. delivered his "I Have a Dream" speech and was the site of President Barack Obama's first presidential inauguration.

    Should the writer make this addition?

    A. Yes, because the additional detail explains why the Lincoln Memorial is so famous.
    B. Yes, because the additional detail proves the significance of the Lincoln Memorial's location.
    C. No, because the additional detail does not support the topic of the paragraph.
    D. No, because the additional detail distracts the reader from the focus of the essay.

Anyone who has seen the movie _Forrest Gump_ will recognize this as the pool through which Jenny waded to reunite with Forrest. (35) If you walk East from the Lincoln Memorial, you encounter the Lincoln Memorial Reflecting Pool. To the left of the Lincoln Memorial you can find the Vietnam Veterans Memorial, located within the Constitution Gardens and to the right lies the Korean War Memorial.

Directly beyond (36) the Reflecting Pool, you can find the World War II Memorial, which consists of wreathed pillars, a fountain, and gold stars that represented (37) all those killed in the war.

Next, the Washington Monument ascends (38) 555 feet into the air, surrounded by U.S. flags.

If you take a left at the Washington Monument, there lays (39) a direct path to the White House, however, (40) if you turn right, you see (41) both the Thomas Jefferson and the Franklin Delano Roosevelt Memorials. If you visit Washington in April, you can see some of the 3,750 cherry trees blossoming.

35. For the sake of logic and coherence, Sentence 1 should be placed:

   A. where it is now
   B. after Sentence 2
   C. after Sentence 3
   D. after Sentence 4

36. A. NO CHANGE
   B. The next stop being
   C. Following
   D. Next,

37. A. NO CHANGE
   B. represent
   C. had represented
   D. are representing

38. Which of the following alternatives to the underlined word would NOT be correct?

   A. rises
   B. reaches
   C. extends
   D. escalates

39. A. NO CHANGE
   B. lies
   C. lay
   D. laid

40. A. NO CHANGE
   B. however,
   C. ; however
   D. ; however,

41. A. NO CHANGE
   B. he or she sees
   C. they see
   D. visitors will see

If you continue toward the Capitol Building, you approach a large carpet of grass and <u>on either side of the grass are located</u> (42) a dozen museums and galleries, including the Smithsonian Natural History Museum, the Air and Space Museum, and the National Gallery of Art.

Finally, situated in front of the U.S. Capitol, <u>is</u> (43) the Ulysses S. Grant Memorial and the Capitol Reflection Pool.

Both the Dome of the Capitol and the Grant Memorial are mirrored beautifully in its <u>surface, which is providing</u> (44) a fitting close to a tourist's walk on the National Mall.

42. A. NO CHANGE
    B. on either side of which are
    C. both sides are in front of
    D. OMIT the underlined portion

43. A. NO CHANGE
    B. was
    C. are
    D. were

44. A. NO CHANGE
    B. surface, and providing
    C. surface which provide
    D. surface; these will provide

45. Suppose the writer's goal had been to write an essay that presents a visual journey from one end of the National Mall to the other. Would this essay successfully fulfill the writer's goal?

    A. No, because the essay limits itself to describing only memorials and monuments.
    B. No, because the essay does not explain where the journey begins and ends.
    C. Yes, because the essay describes a clear progression from the Lincoln Memorial to the Capitol Building.
    D. Yes, because the essay provides exact instructions for what a tourist needs to do to visit the National Mall.

Passage 4: RAGBRAI

Each last week of July, <u>bicyclists, from around the world</u> (46) come to the state of Iowa to participate in a non-competitive bike ride.

Started in 1973 by two *Des Moines Register* newspaper columnists (<u>who thought it would be "interesting" to cycle across the state and write columns along the way</u>) (47), the ride has become an annual event.

RAGBRAI, an acronym for "Register's Annual Great Bicycle Ride Across Iowa," is now both the oldest and the largest <u>efficiently organized</u> (48) bicycle ride in the world.

<u>I grew up in Iowa and RAGBRAI is as old as I am.</u> (49) In the race, Bikers begin on the western border of the state and ride an average of 70 miles a day to reach the Mississippi River on the eastern border. The average length of the race is 472 miles.

46. A. NO CHANGE
    B. bicyclists from around the world,
    C. bicyclists from around the world
    D. bicyclists, from around the world,

47. If the writer were to delete the information inside the parentheses, the essay would primarily lose:

    A. important background information about the origin of RAGBRAI
    B. a detail that provides a logical transition to the remainder of the sentence
    C. the idea that RAGBRAI was invented by two newspaper reporters
    D. nothing of significance because the information is not essential

48. A. NO CHANGE
    B. efficiently and legally organized
    C. official organization
    D. organized

49. Which choice most effectively signals the shift from the preceding paragraph to this paragraph?

    A. NO CHANGE
    B. Each year brings a new, carefully planned route across the state.
    C. Many other states hold similar bicycle rides today, but RAGBRAI was the first.
    D. The first year there were only 300 riders, but the following year there were 1,200.

If the race were in Texas, this distance would be 895 miles. (50) Six designated communities along the route host bikers for the night.

Although the official rider limit is 8,500, many bikers join RAGBRAI along the route up to (51) 10,000 bikers can swarm into a small town for an overnight stay. Tradition dictates that these host communities give the riders food and entertain them.

The summer I turned 15 (52) RAGBRAI came through my small town.

It was a big deal to be selected for an overnight stay—towns competed for the honor—and we had spent a lot of time getting ready. (53)

Riders started arriving at the town square in the early afternoon. The high school band, wearing heavy uniforms, played a raucous rendition of our school fight song.

The volunteer fire department welcomed (54) the riders with twin arches of water spouting high over the road.

Moreover, (55) many townspeople had put up food and drink stands. My friends and I served cookies and orange juice to long lines of hungry and thirsty riders.

50. A. NO CHANGE
    B. Iowa is not as far across as some states are.
    C. (Other states are far larger than Iowa is.)
    D. OMIT the underlined portion.

51. Which of the following alternatives to the underlined portion would NOT be acceptable?

    A. NO CHANGE
    B. route, up to
    C. route, so up to
    D. route; so up to

52. A. NO CHANGE
    B. The summer I turned 15,
    C. The summer I turned 15;
    D. The summer I turned 15:

53. A. NO CHANGE
    B. time thinking and talking about it
    C. weeks preparing for it
    D. most of the summer sorting things out

54. A. NO CHANGE
    B. volunteer fire department, which welcomed
    C. volunteer fire department, welcoming
    D. the volunteer fire department who were welcoming

55. A. NO CHANGE
    B. More important,
    C. As a consequence,
    D. Following tradition,

We ran out of ice immediately <u>almost</u>, (56) but the riders didn't fuss about it.

That night, there <u>was</u> (57) fireworks at the park, and the riders danced to the music played by a local band.

<u>There was a brief rain shower just as the show ended.</u> (58)

We were all up early the next morning to watch the thousands of riders continue <u>their</u> (59) journey toward the Mississippi.

We knew they would uphold the RAGBRAI tradition of dipping their bikes' front tires into the river to mark what they'd already accomplished. (60)

56. The best placement for the underlined word would be:

  A. where it is now.
  B. after the word We.
  C. after the word ice.
  D. after the word were.

57. A. NO CHANGE
  B. were
  C. had been
  D. is

58. Which choice would most effectively introduce the rest of this paragraph?

  A. NO CHANGE
  B. My friends and I had never had so much fun in our lives.
  C. The riders and townspeople alike were exhausted by then and turned in for the night.
  D. None of us were prepared for the sheer number of people at the fairgrounds.

59. A. NO CHANGE
  B. its
  C. his or her
  D. everyone's

60. If the writer were to change the pronoun We to One in the preceding sentence, this closing sentence would:

  A. indicate that the writer has been on RAGBRAI him or herself
  B. suggest that most readers are unaware of the tire-dipping tradition
  C. adopt a more impersonal and objective tone
  D. more likely persuade the reader to participate in RAGBRAI

Passage 5: J.D. Salinger

Jerome David "J.D." Salinger <u>born on January 1, 1919</u> (61) was an American writer best known for one book, *The Catcher in the Rye*, and one character, the profane and troubled Holden Caulfield. (62)

Salinger's fame as the creator of one of youth's enduring icons was something he spent much of his life <u>running away from</u>. (63) He spent the last half of his life in solitude, refusing interviews and declining to have his photograph taken. Salinger died <u>by</u> (64) natural causes in 2010.

As a teen, Salinger was kicked out of several schools because of his poor grades. His parents <u>having sent</u> (65) him to a military school in Pennsylvania, from which he graduated. After that, he returned to New York.

61. A. NO CHANGE
    B. , born on January 1, 1919
    C. , born on January 1, 1919,
    D. born, on January 1, 1919,

62. The writer is considering deleting the phrase "the profane and troubled Holden Caulfield" from the preceding sentence. If the writer were to delete this phrase, the essay would primarily lose:

    A. a minor detail in the introductory paragraph
    B. an identification of the "one character"
    C. an indication of the importance of this character
    D. the writer's opinion about the character

63. A. NO CHANGE
    B. trying not to think about
    C. being resentful of
    D. avoiding

64. A. NO CHANGE
    B. of
    C. through
    D. with

65. A. NO CHANGE
    B. were sending
    C. sent
    D. who sent

ENGLISH EXPRESSION ANSWER KEY

Question #	Correct Answer	Hint
1	C	The placement of an apostrophe in possessive words tells the reader whether the word is singular or plural.
2	D	The words describing the writer's family are set off by punctuation because they are identifying individuals within a unit. Choose your answer based on the entire sentence.
3	B	Choose the answer that keeps the adjectives in parallel form.
4	B	Pay attention to the LEAST in the stem. You're being asked to choose the transitional expression that would NOT work. Try each one in the sentence and check that it's a logical fit.
5	D	Read the choices carefully to choose only the necessary words.
6	A	Here, you need number agreement in two places: the indefinite pronoun—this or these—and in the verb choice. Choose your answer based on the context of the sentence.
7	C	Who is "they?" Is there an antecedent? What is the correct order for two pronouns serving as a compound subject?
8	C	The second half of the sentence should support/explain the first half.
9	D	Read the sentence and decide what information is relevant and non-repetitive.
10	B	Check for sentence completeness.
11	C	Choose the best placement for the comma to ensure understanding and for sentence clarity.
12	A	Modifying phrases should be placed close to the words they're modifying. Decide what the phrase is modifying, and this should lead you to its proper placement.
13	B	Check both punctuation and verb forms for sentence completeness.
14	A	"By the time" affects the verb tense for this sentence.
15	C	A good concluding sentence should end the essay on a satisfying and appropriate note.
16	A	Consider the verb tense established in this sentence. Is it simple past, or is it describing a past action that continues to today?
17	C	Look at the sentence structure—are there two independent clauses or just one?

18	A	Remember that all sentences in a paragraph need to support the main idea of the paragraph.
19	B	Transitional statements should move the reader from the ideas in one paragraph to the ideas in the next.
20	B	When providing a list, all verbs and phrases should be in parallel form.
21	C	An appositive is a phrase that identifies or renames the subject of the sentence and requires specific punctuation.
22	D	Good writing is clear and concise without repetition or excessive wordiness. Which option includes all necessary information most clearly?
23	A	What is the topic of the preceding sentence? Which option best supports that topic?
24	C	Pay attention to the NOT in the stem. Read the sentence and try each answer option to decide which would NOT be logical or appropriate.
25	D	A complete sentence must contain a subject, at least one verb, and express a complete thought.
26	A	Read the entire sentence with each answer option and determine which one has both correct sentence and logical structure.
27	A	Consider the pronoun's antecedent—what is it referring to? Also consider punctuation given there is a comma after "Supreme Court."
28	B	Adverbs can modify verbs. In this case, each adverb is modifying the verb "removed." Which best describes how the Cherokee were removed and marched?
29	B	Pay attention to the NOT in the stem. Read the sentence with each verb form given to discern the verb form that would be incorrect.
30	C	Skim the entire passage to review what it contains. How does it open and how does it close? If you had to state what the passage was about in one sentence, what would you say?
31	D	Check for sentence completeness.
32	B	Always have a reason for a comma. Try to think of a purpose for each comma in both the passage and the answer options.
33	A	Choose the most concise language that states the necessary information.
34	D	Be sure to skim the entire passage to see if the addition of this detail would be consistent with the entire essay.

35	B	Read the entire paragraph so you can choose the most logical placement for the sentence.
36	A	Choose the transitional expression that logically fits and also creates a complete sentence.
37	B	This item addresses verb tense. Check the tense of the sentence and surrounding sentences to arrive at the correct answer.
38	D	Pay attention to the NOT in the stem. You're looking for the word that would NOT be the correct meaning in the context of the sentence.
39	B	Choose the correct verb form—lie or lay—as well as its correct tense given the context of the sentence.
40	D	Punctuation for a conjunctive adverb such as "however" varies depending on the job it is doing in the sentence. Is it connecting two independent clauses or simply interrupting a simple sentence?
41	B	Is a shift in viewpoint appropriate here? Does the verb agree with its subject?
42	B	Choose the wording that is clear, concise, and produces a coherent sentence.
43	C	Identify the subject in this sentence and make certain the verb agrees with it in number and in tense.
44	C	This item addresses the correct way to connect two clauses. Check conjunctions and verb forms for sentence completeness.
45	C	Review the entire essay and decide yes or no. Then look specifically for the reason it either does or does not meet the writer's goal.
46	C	Always have a reason for a comma. Try to think of a purpose for each comma in both the passage and the answer options.
47	D	Writers use parentheses to include additional information. Is this parenthetical information necessary to an understanding of the passage?
48	D	Think carefully about the meanings of each word in the passage and answer options. Which best describes the bicycle ride?
49	B	Choose the sentence that works best as a topic sentence for the paragraph. Check that all other sentences support that topic sentence.
50	D	Ask yourself if this is relevant information at this point in the essay.

51	C	Pay attention to the NOT in the stem. What is the correct structure and punctuation for a compound sentence?
52	B	Consider the correct punctuation for an introductory element.
53	C	Avoid vagueness and unnecessary wordiness in writing. Choose the option that is both clear and concise.
54	A	Check for sentence completeness.
55	D	Transitions move your reader from one idea to the next. Choose the most logical phrase that not only continues from the previous paragraph but also moves most smoothly into the next.
56	C	Adverbs can modify verbs, adjectives, or other adverbs and should remain close to the word they're modifying. Read the sentence and decide which word "almost" is modifying.
57	B	Remember in the present tense, verbs must agree with their subjects in number. Identify the subject of this sentence and that should lead you to the correct verb choice.
58	C	Consider the paragraph as a whole. Trace the chronology of events.
59	A	Find the antecedent for the pronoun in the sentence. Remember pronouns must agree with their antecedents in number, gender, and person.
60	C	Point of view should remain relatively consistent in writing. Think about the difference between a first person account and a third person account of an event.
61	C	Think about both punctuation for a date and punctuation for an explanatory phrase that appears between the subject and the verb of a sentence.
62	B	Think about the detail in the context of the first paragraph. Would an essential meaning be lost if this detail were deleted?
63	D	Good writing uses clear and concise language. Review the options to decide which states the writer's meaning most effectively.
64	B	Preposition with idiomatic language— choose the correct preposition that goes with the saying "died . . . natural causes."
65	C	Check sentence structure—identify the subject of the sentence and this should lead you to the proper answer choice.

BIOGRAPHICAL INFORMATION TEST

These seventy-five multiple-choice questions need to be answered within forty minutes. Don't forget to give examples when asked (in your Word file), and remember that you only get 200 characters per answer. When you're done, check if you've answered every question, haven't skipped giving examples, and haven't given examples longer than 200 characters.

Also, there is no grading sheet for this portion but instead this services as practice and should give you an understanding of the type of questions you will face. After you've finished this section, I would recommend that you go back through and find ways to strengthen your answers.

QUESTIONS

1. How many friends do you have that are from another ethnic background than you are?

    A. 0
    B. 1
    C. 2
    D. 3
    E. More than 3

2. In the last 12 months, how many events did you organize that were attended by more than 10 people?

    A. 0
    B. 1
    C. 2
    D. 3
    E. More than 3

3. How many concerts did you go to in the last 12 months? List examples.

    A. 0
    B. 1
    C. 2
    D. 3
    E. More than 3

4. How often do your colleagues ask you for help when they have difficulties with their work? Give en example of such a situation.

    A. Very often
    B. Often
    C. Sometimes
    D. Seldom
    E. Never

5. How confident are you about your writing style?

    A. Very confident
    B. Rather confident

    C. It's okay

    D. Not that confident

    E. Very insecure

6. How many non-profit or volunteer organizations are you a member of? List them.

    A. 0

    B. 1

    C. 2

    D. 3

    E. More than 3

7. How many countries have you visited in the last 12 months? List them

    A. 0

    B. 1

    C. 2

    D. 3

    E. More than 3

8. Over the last four years, how many classes or courses did you voluntarily (they were not required for your studies or job) take to improve your skills? Give examples.

    A. 0

    B. 1

    C. 2

    D. 3

    E. More than 3

9. In the last three years, how often have you spoken in front of a group of more than 10 people? List examples if you have more than once.

    A. 0

    B. 1–2 times

    C. 3–5 times

    D. 6–10 times

    E. More than 10 times

10. When you are defending an idea or proposal, would your boss, your colleagues or your professors say you are ...

    A. Much more persuasive than other people
    B. Somewhat more persuasive than other people
    C. About as persuasive as other people
    D. Somewhat less persuasive than other people
    E. Not persuasive at all

11. How many times did you act as a leader in college? Give examples.

    A. 0
    B. 1–2 times
    C. 3–5 times
    D. 6–10 times
    E. More than 10 times

12. How often do you send a written thank you note after receiving a present, a favor, or something else?

    A. Very often
    B. Often
    C. Sometimes
    D. Seldom
    E. Never

13. How good would your friends and family say you are at selecting gifts?

    A. Much better than other people
    B. Somewhat better than other people
    C. About as good as other people
    D. Somewhat worse than other people
    E. Much worse than other people

14. How likely are you to ask questions during presentations at school or work?

    A. Much more likely than other people
    B. Somewhat more likely than other people
    C. About as likely as other people
    D. Somewhat less likely than other people
    E. Much less likely than other people

15. How many positions of leadership did you hold in college?

    A. 0
    B. 1
    C. 2
    D. 3
    E. More than 3

16. How often do people ask you for help with computer problems?

    A. Very often
    B. Often
    C. Sometimes
    D. Seldom
    E. Never

17. How many movies did you see in the last 6 months? List examples

    A. 0
    B. 1–3
    C. 4–6
    D. 7–9
    E. More than 9

18. How would your colleagues, supervisors, or professors rate your ability to properly analyze a problem?

    A. Much better than that of other people
    B. Better than that of other people
    C. About the same as that of other people
    D. Worse than that of other people
    E. Much worse than that of other people

19. How likely are you to take responsibility for a project or task at school or at work?

    A. Much more likely than other people
    B. Somewhat more likely than other people
    C. About as likely as other people
    D. Somewhat less likely than other people
    E. Much less likely than other people

20. Did you graduate from college with any honors? Which ones? If you answer E, please explain.

    A. None
    B. Cum Laude
    C. Magna Cum Laude
    D. Summa Cum Laude
    E. Other

21. How many magazines do you read on a frequent basis? List examples.

    A. 0
    B. 1
    C. 2
    D. 3
    E. More than 3

22. How often do you read articles about technology?

    A. Very often
    B. Often
    C. Sometimes
    D. Seldom
    E. Never

23. Before giving a presentation to a large group, will you practice it aloud in front by yourself or in front of someone else?

    A. Yes, very often
    B. Yes, often
    C. Yes, sometimes
    D. Yes, but seldom
    E. No, never

24. How often do you attend events where you know nobody?

    A. Very often
    B. Often
    C. Sometimes
    D. Seldom
    E. Never

25. Have you held any of the following positions during your educational career: teaching assistant, student council, work-study program, resident advisor or assistant, varsity team? How many?

    A. 0
    B. 1
    C. 2
    D. 3
    E. More than 3

26. How many friends do you have with a different religious background than yours?

    A. 0
    B. 1
    C. 2
    D. 3
    E. More than 3

27. How creative do your colleagues, supervisors, or professors think you are in solving problems?

    A. Much more creative than other people
    B. Somewhat more creative than other people
    C. About as creative as other people
    D. Somewhat less creative than other people
    E. Much less creative than other people

28. How intimidating do you find it to start a conversation with a person you don't know?

    A. Very intimidating
    B. More intimidating than other people
    C. About as intimidating as other people
    D. Less intimidating than other people
    E. Not intimidating at all

29. How many meetings did you lead in the last 12 months? List examples

    A. 0
    B. 1–2
    C. 3–4

    D. 5–6

    E. More than 6

30. How effective would your colleagues, superiors, or professors say you are at using appropriate humor?

    A. Much more effective than other people

    B. Somewhat more effective than other people

    C. About as effective as other people

    D. Somewhat less effective than other people

    E. Much less effective than other people

31. How many countries have you visited for work or for your studies in the last 12 months?

    A. 0

    B. 1

    C. 2

    D. 3

    E. More than 3

32. Are you anxious when you need to speak in front of a large group?

    A. Very much

    B. Much

    C. Some

    D. A little

    E. Very little

33. How good are you at creatively solving problems? Give examples.

    A. Better than most people

    B. Somewhat better than most people

    C. About as good as other people

    D. Somewhat worse than other people

    E. Worse than other people

34. How many countries have you lived in for more than 60 consecutive days?

    A. 0

    B. 1

C. 2

D. 3

E. More than 3

35. How comfortable are you interacting with people from a different ethnic background than yours?

    A. Much more comfortable than other people

    B. Somewhat more comfortable than other people

    C. About as comfortable as other people

    D. Somewhat less comfortable than other people

    E. Much less comfortable than other people

36. How many books have you read in the last 24 months? List examples.

    A. 0

    B. 1–3

    C. 4–6

    D. 7–9

    E. More than 9

37. How many different U.S. states have you lived in for the last seven years? List examples.

    A. 1

    B. 2

    C. 3

    D. 4

    E. More than 4

38. How many letters have you written to magazines or newspapers in reply to a published article? List the topics and publications.

    A. 0

    B. 1

    C. 2

    D. 3

    E. More than 3

39. How many of those letters were published? List the topics and publications.

    A. 0

    B. 1

    C. 2

    D. 3

    E. More than 3

40. How many of your college, job, or volunteer functions require you to organize events for more than 10 people? List examples.

    A. 0

    B. 1

    C. 2

    D. 3

    E. More than 3

41. In how many languages can you write effortlessly? List examples.

    A. 0

    B. 1

    C. 2

    D. 3

    E. More than 3

42. How many hobbies do you practice on at least a monthly basis? Give examples.

    A. 0

    B. 1

    C. 2

    D. 3

    E. More than 3

43. How likely are you to stay in touch with former classmates or colleagues?

    A. Much more likely than other people

    B. Somewhat more likely than other people

    C. About as likely as other people

    D. Somewhat less likely than other people

    E. Much less likely than other people

44. How many continents did you visit in the last 12 months? List them.

    A. 0
    B. 1
    C. 2
    D. 3
    E. More than 3

45. How often do you create task lists for yourself?

    A. Very often
    B. Often
    C. Sometimes
    D. Seldom
    E. Never

46. In the last year, how often did you volunteer to help out with a task that wasn't your responsibility? List examples.

    A. 0
    B. 1
    C. 2
    D. 3
    E. More than 3

47. How often do people ask you for book recommendations?

    A. Very often
    B. Often
    C. Sometimes
    D. Seldom
    E. Never

48. How many friends do you have in other countries that are not expats? List the countries.

    A. 0
    B. 1
    C. 2
    D. 3
    E. More than 3

49. How often do your colleagues ask you for help with problems they're facing outside of work?

    A. Very often
    B. Often
    C. Sometimes
    D. Seldom
    E. Never

50. In the last year, how many sports teams have you played with? List examples

    A. 0
    B. 1
    C. 2
    D. 3
    E. More than 3

51. How would people around you rate your capability to explain complex matters in a simple way?

    A. Much more capable than other people
    B. Somewhat more capable than other people
    C. About as capable as other people
    D. Somewhat less capable than other people
    E. Much less capable than other people

52. How much do you love learning new skills or improving skills that you already have? List some skills that you have learned or improved upon in the last year.

    A. I love it much more than other people do
    B. I love it more than other people do
    C. I love it such as much as other people do
    D. I love it a little less than other people do
    E. I don't love it nearly as much as other people do

53. How many friends do you have whose first language is not English?

    A. 0
    B. 1
    C. 2
    D. 3

E. More than 3

54. How many theater plays or dance performances have you attended in the last year? List them.

    A. 0
    B. 1
    C. 2
    D. 3
    E. More than 3

55. How many awards or other official signs of recognition have you received in the last 24 months? List examples

    A. 0
    B. 1
    C. 2
    D. 3
    E. More than 3

56. How many books did you read in the last 24 months that were in another language than English? Give examples.

    A. 0
    B. 1
    C. 2
    D. 3
    E. More than 3

57. If you come up with solutions for a problem, would people describe them as "out of the box?"

    A. Usually, yes
    B. Often, yes
    C. Sometimes, yes
    D. Rarely
    E. Never

58. How often do you ask your colleagues for help at work?

    A. Very often

    B. Often

    C. Sometimes

    D. Seldom

    E. Never

59. How well do you keep up with the latest technologies?

    A. Very well

    B. Rather well

    C. As well as most other people

    D. Not so well

    E. Not well at all

60. Which of the following newspaper sections interests you most?

    A. Business

    B. International news

    C. National news

    D. Opinion/editorial

    E. Sports

61. How capable would others say you are at resolving conflicts between colleagues, friends, family members, etc.?

    A. Much more capable than other people

    B. Somewhat more capable than other people

    C. About as capable as other people

    D. Somewhat less capable than other people

    E. Much less capable than other people

62. How often do you ask colleagues about their personal lives?

    A. Very often

    B. Often

    C. Sometimes

    D. Seldom

    E. Never

63. How many times a month do you go meet up with friends, on average? List some things you regularly do with them.

    A. 0
    B. 1
    C. 2
    D. 3
    E. More than 3

73. How often are you nervous before a long trip?

    A. Very often
    B. Often
    C. Sometimes
    D. Seldom
    E. Never

74. How confident do your supervisors, colleagues, or professors think you are?

    A. Much more self-confident than he should be
    B. Somewhat more self-confident than he should be
    C. Appropriately confident
    D. Somewhat less self-confident than he should be
    E. Much less self-confident than he should be

75. How many non-work-related leadership positions have you held in the last 12 months?

    A. 0
    B. 1
    C. 2
    D. 3
    E. More than 3

ESSAY EXERCISE

When you practice the essay, try to finish within twenty-five minutes (you'll get thirty at the FSOT, but you'll be nervous). There's no answer key for this exercise, but below the essay, I'll tell you what your essay should definitely include. Set your timer, open your "FSOT Practice Essay" Word file, take your notepad for scratch paper (one sheet!), and go!

ESSAY PROMPT

Euthanasia is a highly debated subject. Some believe doctors should only help prolong life and not end it, while others feel that people should have the right to end their lives with the right help. Even in the pro-camp, there is discussion, as some feel that euthanasia is only acceptable if the asking party is suffering deeply either mentally or physically, while others don't want to put restrictions on the practice. In your opinion, should euthanasia be allowed and, if so, under which limitations, if any? Support your opinion with two facts.

ESSAY "MUSTS"

Use this checklist to determine whether your essay includes all the necessary elements:

- An introduction introducing the thesis
- Arguments for your opinion, supported by two facts
- Possible counter-arguments that you refute
- A conclusion that briefly summarizes what you stated before

RESOURCES

In this penultimate chapter, I want to give you some useful resources. These are books and websites that offer insight into becoming and being an FSO, as well as information straight from the State Department, **but they are not study material**. As I mentioned, you should be just fine if you stick to the study material listed in the Recommended Reading chapter. Of course, that's not to say you can't find some handy things in the list below.

General information

http://careers.state.gov/work/foreign-service/officer/test-process: An official overview of the entire FSOT selection process by the Department of State. I've actually included much more information in this book—you won't find any secret tips on the state.gov site. But the infographic they created is pretty cool and gives you a clear overview of the process.

http://careerbrochures.state.gov/fsofssbrochures/fscareers?pg=1: This brochure by the Department of State contains about the same information as the page above, but you can print it out, which might make it a better option if you're more of a paper person.

Eligibility

http://careers.state.gov/uploads/fd/3c/fd3c2fd3136c4acc72908390f0c2dd39/three_con ditions_fsemployment.pdf: You will need to sign this form if you want to become an FSO, so better have a look at it before starting the process.

Security check

http://careers.state.gov/uploads/8f/f7/8ff7b0bab879946e78f30e62c859c0f1/DualCitizen ship.pdf: This document contains information for U.S. citizens who have dual citizenship and want to become an FSO. Be sure to check this before applying.

www.freecreditreport.com: This site allows you to download your credit report for free once a year. Make sure to check it and report any errors to Experian, Transunion, or Equifax.

Career track selection

http://careers.state.gov/work/foreign-service/officer/career-tracks: The official State Department's overview of the different career tracks. This page is interesting because of the links to interviews with actual FSOs who work in the different career tracks and talk about their jobs.

http://careers.state.gov/work/foreign-service/officer/career-track-quiz: A fun quiz by the Department of State to guide you in your career track choice. I do think you should make this decision by yourself and use this test more as a way to confirm your decision or help you choose between two tracks. Don't let it make the decision for you. Also, if you use this to help make your choice, don't tell the board on your FSOA interview when they ask why you chose a specific career. That will look negatively upon you.

Registering for the FSOT

http://pearsonvue.com/fsot/: Pearson VUE is the company organizing the FSOT, so this is where you need to go for information on testing dates and locations. Be sure to check this page as the registration process changed on September 30, 2015. You don't want to get confused by older information you may find on the Internet.

Studying for the FSOT

Job Knowledge

http://www.economist.com/economist-quiz: *The Economist* runs a weekly quiz on current affairs. It's fun to do while still studying.

http://www.sheppardsoftware.com/Geography.htm: Take these geography quizzes to make sure you don't just know all about a country's economy, social system, and conflict history, but also ... where it's actually located. You'd be surprised how many times you can answer a question just by knowing who is a surrounding country.

http://www.mathopolis.com/questions/quizzes.php: Math quizzes on different subjects and for different levels. Just in case you want to train your internal calculator some more.

English Expression

http://www.actstudent.org/sampletest/english/eng_01.html: ACT organized the FSOT before Pearson VUE did, so this English practice exam is great if you want to take another one on top of the two in this book and the official one by the State Department.

Essay

http://www.actstudent.org/writing/sample/: ACT also offers a sample essay prompt followed by sample essays. What's useful is that each sample essay is graded and accompanied by an in-depth explanation of why it's graded the way it is. Remember that ACT was in charge of the FSOT before Pearson VUE and the grading did not change much.

http://education.depaul.edu/student-resources/academic-success-center/Documents/501writingprompts.pdf: As the title says, these are 501 essay prompts to help you practice your essay writing skills. The topics are very diverse, so you can practice with things you find easy to write about and things you may have more difficulty forming an opinion on.

Training material by the Department of State

http://careers.state.gov/connect/events: A list of training events organized by the Department of State. There are events for the FSOT but also for the FSOA. I've never been to one, as I didn't feel it was necessary, but I've heard from others that they found it useful to have a kind of "class" moment to ask questions and make the test more real as opposed to when it was just them and their books studying at home.

Department of State App: Contains information about the Foreign Service including a handy FAQ section. Even more interesting are probably the practice tests. They give you a good idea of the kind of questions you can expect on the FSOT. A bit of a downside to these test questions is also that the app only tells you if you got them wrong or right but not why you got them wrong or right.

iTunes: https://itunes.apple.com/us/app/doscareers/id580287301?mt=8

Android: https://play.google.com/store/apps/details?id=com.metrostarsystems.fsc.android

http://careers.state.gov/fsopracticetest/: The Department of State has two official practice tests. However, you have to wait for six months after you've taken the first one to be able to take the second one; otherwise, the website will just give you the first one again. So if you plan to study for the FSOT for longer than six months in total, I recommend you take the first practice test as soon as possible and then the second one after you've thoroughly studied and should be ready for the exam. If your study period is shorter than six months, though, just take the one practice test before going to the FSOT. A downside to the official practice test is that it only contains the Job Knowledge and an English Expression portion of the test. There are no Biographical Information Test questions or essay prompts.

http://www.careers.state.gov/uploads/4c/e8/4ce8ce99d45087fc22dbd582ebab88f7/3.0.0 _FSO_13_dimensions.pdf: This PDF on the thirteen dimensions of a great FSO is not meant as a training tool, but I advise you to print it out and keep it close when you're preparing for the biographical section of the test and later for the QEP and the FSOA. That way you can make sure your answers are in line with what the Department of State is looking for—but keep it honest!

Groups, forums, and experts

https://groups.yahoo.com/neo/groups/fswe/info: The Yahoo FSOT group was started in 2003, and ever since then, FSOT candidates have been exchanging study tips and test experiences on there. It's *the* place to discuss any uncertainties you might have and form study groups with other candidates.

https://www.reddit.com/r/foreignservice/: Newer than the Yahoo group is the Foreign Service subreddit. The topics in here are very diverse and go from addressing particular points of the FSOT to practical questions about being an FSO and relevant current affairs.

http://careers.state.gov/connect/forums/foreign-service-forums: The official Department of State FS forums are where you want to ask technical and practical questions related to the FSOT. Those will be answered clearly by government officials, but this is not the best place to discuss studying tactics and past test experiences.

http://careers.state.gov/connect/dir: This is a list of the Diplomats in Residence (DIR) and their contact information. It allows you to contact diplomats all over the U.S. who are specialized in giving career advice. If you really want to know what life as an FSO is like, or unsure about whether it's for you, these are the people you want to talk to. However, in most cases, they will not help to prepare you for the FSOT.

The FSOA

http://careers.state.gov/uploads/c0/57/c05721f7f261f40aa69e142cd888c5a8/What-to-Bring-to-OA-9-2015.pdf: A list of things to bring with you on the day of the FSOA.

On life in the Foreign Service

"Inside a U.S. embassy": This book provides thorough information about the day-to-day day business at U.S. embassies all over the world. It's a great read both before taking the test—to make sure you actually want to do what the people in these embassies are doing—and after the test—to prepare yourself for what's coming next.

http://www.afsa.org/foreign-service-blogs: a list of blogs kept by Foreign Service Officers. Although you might find references to the FSOT on some of these blogs, they're mostly interesting because they offer a window into the lives of actual FSOs. AFSA, by the way, is the American Foreign Service Association and offers lots of practical information for FSOs like how to move abroad with a pet.

Extra: a handy app

Evernote: Evernote lets you organize, notes, images, online articles, and more in notes and notebooks. It's ideal for collecting and structuring information you get from reading newspapers, for example. You could make a notebook per country, conflict, or event, and simply save all the information you come across on the topic to review later. I still use Evernote today to create dossiers on certain topics so that it's easy for me to quickly retrieve information on them when needed.

Made in the USA
Middletown, DE
23 March 2016